The Author

Lindsay Jenkins is an investigative author and journalist. She specialises in the history and current operations of the European Union. She formerly worked for British and American investment banks in the City of London and as a senior civil servant in the British Ministry of Defence. She received an honours degree in mediaeval and modern history from Bedford College, London University and an MBA from Cranfield School of Management. She lives in both the UK and US.

Britain in Europe

Disappearing Britain is the third volume in the
continuing series

Available in this series
by the same author

Britain Held Hostage, The Coming Euro-Dictatorship

The Last Days of Britain, The Final Betrayal

www.lindsayjenkins.com

DISAPPEARING BRITAIN

The EU and the
Death of Local Government

LINDSAY JENKINS

Orange State Press
Washington D.C.

First published in 2005 by Orange State Press

A division of Orange State Communications
PO Box 1851
New York NY 10150-1851
USA

www.orangestatepress.com

UK distributor
The June Press
www.junepress.com

ISBN 0–9657812–3–2

British Library cataloguing in Publication Data
A catalogue record for this book is avilable from the British Library.

Phototypeset in 10¼ pt on 13¼ pt Linotron Sabon by Intype Libra Ltd
Printed in Great Britain by Biddles Ltd

Original cover by Alice Leach
www.aliceleach.com

Contents

CONTENTS

Acknowledgements

Many people have contributed to this book and I am grateful to each every one of them.

I would especially like to thank Nigel Farage MEP for information that I would otherwise have had grave difficulty uncovering, for his consistent encouragement and for his determination to 'out' the truth.

I owe a debt of gratitude to Geoffrey Collier; Jane de Rome; Nigel Draper; the Rev. Philip Foster; Neil Herron; Richard Hill; Rodney Howlett; Greg Lance-Watkins; Mrs Joan Martin, Peter Martin-Kaye; Cdr Bryan G Smalley RD DL; Ronald Stewart-Brown; Horst Teubert; the Hon. Neil Turner OBE DL; Peter Watson; George West; Roger Wilson; Cllr Tony Woodcock; and Bill and Ann Woodhouse.

Dr Anthony Martin has edited this book with erudition, perspicacity and stringency. Any errors that may remain are my own.

Again the staff of the London Library was peerless.

The Foreword
by
. Norman Tebbit

Lindsay Jenkins' meticulous research has uncovered in all its details the Brussels Eurocrats' agenda for the break up of the United Kingdom. There is nothing secret in what she has exposed, but she is the first to put together the many pieces in this jigsaw to reveal the full picture of the plan, which will shock many people.

England, and later the United Kingdom, has been the rock on which every attempt to create a European wide state has foundered since the collapse of the Roman Empire. The contemporary hostility of the European establishment towards the Anglo sphere has been built on the historic European ambition that powered Philip of Spain, Napoleon Bonaparte, the Kaiser and Hitler to create their European empires. Even today the would-be imperialists who dream of challenging America for world leadership know that until this Kingdom is subdued their ambition will not be achieved.

That is at the heart of the plan, which Lindsay Jenkins exposes. With the enthusiastic backing of Prime Minister Blair 300 years of union with Scotland is being undone. Wales is being pushed away and IRA/Sinn Fein is not being so much appeased as treated like an ally in the destruction of the United Kingdom.

Even so that is not enough. What New Labour pretends is devolution to the English regions, Lindsay Jenkins shows step by step is a plan from Brussels to take England back to its state before the time of Alfred the Great, divided and incapable of resisting foreign colonisation. Westminster is being by-passed.

The Regions are encouraged to deal bilaterally with Brussels, softened with sweet talk and expensive lunches to be integrated as regions into a European Union not of sovereign states but dependent provinces.

Far fetched? Well, read the book. There is no need to assess Lindsay Jenkins' opinions. Just look at the documented facts and judge for yourself. Step by step, year by year, this books sets out how Parliament and constitutional Monarchy, long the epitome of democratic practice, are being sidelined by the creation of regional government. Unlike our Parliament and Monarchy this is not growing organically in response to changing times and changing needs. It is being built to a master plan devised by foreign interests not to strengthen but to neuter this country and eliminate any focal point of opposition to Imperial Europe. It is being implemented step by step to avoid the public resistance were its purpose to be known.

This book echoes Gladstone's speech at Hastings on 17th March 1891.

'No violence, no tyranny, whether of experiments or of such methods as are likely to be made in this country, could ever for a moment have a chance of prevailing against the energies of that great Assembly (The House of Commons),

> "No; if these powers of the House of Commons come to be encroached upon, it will be by tacit and insidious methods, and therefore I say that public attention should be called to this."'

Lindsay Jenkins' book 'calls attention to this'.

London
July 2005

Introducing the Slow Death of Nations and Democracy

This is the post democratic era
This is the story of how and why nationhood and democracy in Britain and across Europe is being overwhelmed by the so-called *post democratic era*. It is a story of deceit and double speaking.

The tide of regional government in the UK has risen fast. Today 22,000 elected local councillors battle 60,000 members of quangos, quasi government agencies funded by the government but nominally independent. These state apparatchiks, embedded in local government, many representing their own wallets, distort democracy.

Control by unelected bureaucrats and by lobby groups behind closed doors is praised in the European Union's capital, Brussels. This *cohesion policy*, says Brussels, is our future.

Spin and propaganda are critical. Time and again institutions and organisations are said to 'have been founded'. They have arisen. No individuals have apparently been involved. Yet in this truly secular enterprise immaculate creation is more than unlikely.

The EU, a single socialist country in the making, already dominates the legislatures of its member countries, spewing out regulations and directives and trampling democracy underfoot. Jacques Delors once boasted that over 80 per cent of legislation would one day come from Europe's 'embryonic government' in Brussels.[1] That day has already arrived.[2] No wonder voters feel alienated and disinclined to vote

Were the EU Constitution to be ratified, the situation would worsen at once. The EU would then have legal identity and EU law would reign supreme over all its constituent provinces. Remaining checks and balances would be so limited as to make that supremacy virtually untrammelled power. Even without a formal constitution, the Franco-German axis and its supporters are already widening the EU's powers.

A plea for local democracy and less government
In highlighting this dire state of governance and the underhand way in which it has been introduced, this book is a plea for local democracy and for less government, for the freedom of the British people to run their own lives in their own country. It is not enough to move government to a town hall near you; the heavy all-encompassing government described in this book must be sharply cut back. It is a plea that has been repeatedly made from Adam Smith to Friedrich Hayek. It remains largely unheeded.

Ironically socialists who despise feudal or class systems are today the source of the new governing class, a bloated bureaucracy, demanding that helpless citizens pay ever more taxes to fuel it, a huge centrifugal power, sucking everything into a black hole.

The effect of this bloated bureaucracy is pernicious. Tax Freedom Day, the day each year when the British start working for themselves and not for the government, is now 31st May, according to the Adam Smith Institute.[3] Year by year the Day falls later and later.

The UK is travelling fast in the wrong direction, towards

bigger and oppressive government, toward the EU. In the Eurozone, Tax Freedom Day does not come until 28 June, a whole month after Britain's. Half the year working for your lord.

But the American Tax Freedom Day is 11 April: 78 more days of freedom for Americans than for people in the euro-zone. Those extra days during which Americans can work for themselves and their families precisely illustrate the difference between one of the world's freest countries and the sclerotic European Union.

British local government is no longer local: it is largely funded by the central government in London. Voting in local elections is nearly meaningless when councillors are not finan-cially accountable to the voter, need not be efficient, and work to a central government agenda. At one public meeting coun-cillors dismissed a local taxpayer who protested about a coun-cil scheme, as usual backed by a chorus of locals with their businesses beholden to that council. The councillors claimed,

'We don't have to take any notice of you. Our money comes from London.'[4]

That direct link between the voter and the elected councillor is now blurred to the point of obscurity. Transparency and accountability, clearly seeing who does what, have gone too.

Now a blanket of regions, sub regions and sub sub regions is cutting off the flame of remaining freedoms.

Party confusion

The three main British political parties have lazily allowed themselves to be absorbed into the regional system.

Liberal Democrats embrace both 'local democracy' and the European Union, yet the two are mutually exclusive. They make no attempt to square the circle.

The Labour Party trumpets its belief in 'good services', but the reality is that it wants to entrench itself in perpetual power. Overwhelmingly defeated in the only referendum on elected regional assemblies, John Prescott, Labour's Deputy Prime Minister, turned on the proverbial sixpence. He abandoned his campaign for elected regional assemblies and immediately claimed that the future of local government now lay with local people. Prescott says he wants *neighbourhoods*, the new word for parishes, to raise and run their own finances.[5]

This tactic may look like a U-turn but looks deceive. It is part of the same agenda. Stopped, at least for the moment, from giving a fig leaf of democracy to regional assemblies, Prescott said he would begin consultations *at once* to create a new breed of 'super mayors' with new powers over transport and regeneration. He wants 'a European approach to creating sustainable communities.' In his characteristically off-key English, he told a Delivering Sustainable Communities Summit in Manchester that

> 'We want people to help share the local public servic-
> es they receive and we want them to become more
> involved in the democratic life of their community. By
> action at a neighbourhood level people everywhere
> can make a significant difference to the quality of our
> country's public services.'[6]

Neighbourhoods are to be given budgets to manage just a few services directly. They might even be allowed to own and manage playgrounds and community centres, and use so-called *triggers* to force the local council to improve failing services. *How To* guides, printed at a cost to the public of £5 million ($8m), will help local people and authorities spend more effectively.[7]

The truth is that the EU's writ circumscribes every policy emanating from the Office of the UK's Deputy Prime Minister.

It would be more accurate to call it the EU Commission's London office with John Prescott as the EU's enforcer.

The Conservative Party has pledged to abolish regional assemblies and other regional quangos – but not all of them.

John Redwood, as Shadow Secretary of State for Deregulation, stated,

> 'We will be abolishing the unelected Regional Assemblies in England, Regional Housing Boards, strategic health authorities and other regional quangos. We are not currently planning to abolish the GLA [the Greater London Assembly]: both the GLA and the Mayor are elected, and were endorsed by the people of London in a referendum, which puts them into a different category.'[8]

Conservative Party thinking is muddled, reflecting a lack of understanding of the source and purpose of regional assemblies. For example, although the GLA is indeed elected, though by proportional representation, the assembly members have no powers, as this book will show. The Labour government rushed through this revolution: the public was allowed only a derisory period to debate the issue of an assembly for London (and Wales) and then barely a quarter of the electorates voted for change.

Is that a truly democratic endorsement, which a Conservative government should uphold? Should a minority be able to impose a fundamental constitutional change on the majority?

There can be no Conservative revival as the party of government if it does not champion national independence, local democracy and smaller government.

The grass roots rebels

British voters are beginning to rebel. According to a review of the letters pages in all local newspapers across the country, the top targets for complaint are local councils. The reviewer commented,

> 'People are absolutely furious with their councils: lack of service, delivery, council tax and especially the huge salaries being paid to council executives. Library and school closures are the main bones of contention.'[9]

High on the list of strident objections were regional assemblies, even though the letter writers were largely unaware of the ramifications of those assemblies. The Labour government's highhanded dismissal of local opinion about housing and shopping complexes is causing enormous anger.

A month after the only referendum in England on an elected regional assembly, a local paper carried the headline *Turmoil At Yorkshire Assembly As Council Quits*. East Riding councillors launched a scathing attack on the regional assembly, complaining of 'pointless meetings with people justifying their own existence'. The £87,500 of council tax-payers' money paid every year to the assembly was being squandered on a talking shop, they said.[10]

That publicity alerted other councils to review their membership of regional assemblies.

Two county councils in the Northwest Region then withdrew from their assembly: the Conservative led Cheshire County Council and the Labour led Lancashire County Council shortly followed by the Conservative controlled Trafford Council.[11] Macclesfield, Ribble Valley and Fylde Councils have also announced their withdrawal.

Rebellion is spreading.

The battle for Britain is now being fought – not at the

national level – but by ordinary people agitating at the grass-roots. That truly is local democracy at work.

This book is intended to give ammunition to the rebels and to alert everyone to the truth behind regional government.

CHAPTER 1

Voters Resoundingly Reject Regional Government

A lot of hot air

On 5th November 2004, the No campaigners triumphantly let the air out of their inflatable white elephant, a potent symbol of their battle for votes. Voters had said an overwhelming No to an elected regional assembly in the North East of England. The No campaign decisively won the argument. Their slogan *Politicians Talk, We Pay* convinced voters that the regional assembly was nothing but a talking shop. An elected regional assembly would be expensive, powerless and remote. A white elephant indeed. And all this despite the fact that the government thought the North East was the one region in England most likely to say Yes.[1]

It was a David versus Goliath battle. The No campaign, an amalgam of Conservatives, the UK Independence Party and independents, had little more than the required £100,000 ($185,000) government grant to spend. Yet it defeated the combined ranks of the Labour government, the Liberal Democrats and the BBC, together spending several million pounds of taxpayers' money. Plenty of local councillors hoping to enjoy larger salaries and expenses, and other well-known local figures aspiring to well-paid jobs for doing little, were

9

very willing to speak to the media praising a regional assembly.

Peter Hain, Labour's Leader of the House of Commons and Welsh Secretary, had urged voters to

> 'Think big and bold about the future of a regional assembly and not worry about the "few extra bob" it will cost to run it . . . This is petty cash compared with the big picture of building a stronger economy and bringing extra social benefits . . . people should use the experience of Wales as proof of the success of devolution'[2]

The people of the North East chose not to emulate Wales and the statistics said it all.

Nearly half the 1.9 million electors in the Northeast voted on the question *Should there be an elected assembly for the North East region?* This was the first all postal ballot in the UK, a government initiative to ensure a large vote despite fears of fraud. Yet postal votes did nothing to help the government's position. 78 per cent voted No. All 23 council areas in the North East voted No. The Nos won by 696,519 votes to 197,310.

The Deputy Prime Minister, John Prescott, confirmed that

> 'the result of the referendum means that the Regional Assemblies Bill will not be introduced in the coming Session of Parliament; under existing legislation, there can be no further referendum on regional assemblies in the North East for at least seven years.'[3]

So that should have been that for at least the next seven years.

Did the No vote really win?

All is not necessarily what it seems.

For a start the campaign was not really about the question on the ballot paper. Voters were asked should there or should there not be an *elected* assembly. But the campaign was fought on the obvious question of should there be an assembly at all. Most voters putting their cross on the ballot paper were probably voting for or against the very existence of a regional assembly.

Voting made no difference. The unelected North East Regional Assembly will continue just as it has since 1999, even though that is probably not want voters really wanted. They were not given the right choice to make.

At no time has the issue of regional assemblies, yes or no, been put to the voters.

Reacting to the referendum result, Nick Raynsford, the Minister for Local and Regional Government said that while the Government would reflect before making decisions about devolution in other regions, he hinted that the Labour Party would return to the regional agenda after the 2005 general election.

John Prescott echoed him in the House of Commons,

> 'It is worth remembering that proposals for Scottish and Welsh devolution failed to win public support in the first referendum in 1979, only for the situation to be reversed 20 years later in a new referendum.'[4]

The Office of the Deputy Prime Minister declares on its website,

> '. . . the Government continues to have a clear policy to decentralise power and improve performance through reform in local government and strengthening all the English regions.'[5]

The government stated that 'future legislation would need to be more ambitious than the Draft Regional Assemblies Bill in order to create regional bodies that are fit for purpose.'[6]

Nick Raynsford wrote to the English Regions Network to counter any suggestion that a No vote on elected regional assemblies might mean a question mark over their future. He said that this 'reflects a misunderstanding both of the role of the existing assemblies and our proposals for elected assemblies.' Emphasising that 'we remain firmly committed to a regional dimension' he went on

> 'We expect the role and responsibilities of regional assemblies to continue to evolve. The consultation exercise on merging regional housing and planning board has just ended. As part of the Pre-budget report on 2 December [2004] we issued a consultation document on proposals for regional funding allocations.'[7]

These are strong hints indeed that the battle will be resumed for elected regional assemblies and next time the Assemblies may be given more authority and thus a greater aura of legitimacy.

'There has to be a regional dimension'

When Michael Howard, the Conservative leader, challenged the Prime Minister to abolish regional assemblies which 'have no popular support at all', Tony Blair retorted

> 'We will not abolish them . . .

> 'The fact of the matter is that they most certainly do serve a purpose, but the reason why the previous Government established the Government offices for the regions is that they recognised that there had to

be a regional dimension. That is precisely what we have recognised with the regional chambers. There will not be a regional assembly in the North East, because they did not vote for one. What will remain are the Government offices for the regions and the regional chambers.'[8]

Tony Blair was playing semantics: regional chambers and regional assemblies are to all intents and purposes the same thing. Despite such a lack of support that two referendums had to be abandoned and a huge win for the No vote in the North East, regions and regional government will continue as before. There will be no change. The voters have no influence.

British regions or EU regions?

No government minister, Conservative or Labour, has ever said in so many words that there is a connection between regions and the EU. The closest any of them came to such an admission was Tony Blair's elliptical statement that for reasons he chose not to disclose regions have to be.

Singing from a different hymn sheet, his Deputy John Prescott has claimed that regions are his idea. He has been working on regions for the last thirty years. The British media and MPs have repeatedly, and largely uncritically, echoed him.

The Labour MEP, Richard Corbett, tried to trounce the idea that the EU is enforcing regional assemblies to divide and rule. He claimed that

'a letter writing campaign to newspapers by UKIP/BNP has caused many to believe this particular myth, but in fact devolution to Scotland, Wales and possibly the English regions is entirely an internal matter for the UK. The EU has no power to decide on the internal structure of individual governments – even if it had, why would it want to?'[9]

Suspecting that regional government might not be a British solution to a British problem, journalists have challenged the EU Commission's office in London that there must be a EU connection.

The Commission has struggled to come up with a plausible rebuttal. It insists that the EU has had nothing to do with the creation of regions or regional government. That is a myth. It argues that Britain had regions during World War II and today's regions continue that purely British initiative.[10] Members of the English regional assemblies say the same thing to deflect charges of EU connections.[11]

That is a false argument. The English Commissions were for civil defence only and never a replacement for local democratic government. Devised in wartime, each Commission was intended to run autonomously should Germany invade, as seemed very likely in the summer of 1940. The Commissions continued for several decades after the war in plans for civil defence. There were ten of these regional seats of government, and they did not have the same boundaries as today's eight regions.

The Labour government obfuscates

The Labour government has repeatedly emphasised that regions are the *devolution* of central government *to the people* as though this were something new. That clever word devolution suggests it is a good thing: reducing opaque and distant central government, increasing local democracy, and giving more power to local people.

Devolution is nothing new. For centuries all British local government has been devolved government. Devolved government is defined by statute law. Local powers can and have been broadened or narrowed by acts of parliament. They can even be abolished.

This contrasts with a federal system, where regional administrations have a constitutionally guaranteed right to exist, with constitutionally defined powers, like the states in the US. An incoming American administration cannot simply change the powers of states like California, Florida or Massachusetts, or even their very existence, by passing a Bill.

So the government's implied argument that devolution is new is specious. The regions are simply large conglomerations of local government: the exact opposite of what the government claims.

John Prescott MP, Richard Corbett MEP, the Labour government and the European Commission are all wrong, as the next chapters will show.

So what is regional government? Why did Tony Blair say that we have to have it? Why can't we get rid of it? Why are the English assemblies operating without elections and without democratic legitimacy? Would elections make any difference?

Are they really British? What more is likely to happen?

CHAPTER 2

The EU Defines Regional Government

In the treaty of Rome

If neither the Deputy Prime Minister, John Prescott, nor the British government nor British civil defence is the source of regions and regional government, then who or what is?

The answer is simple. The legal source of regional economic government is the 1957 treaty of Rome.

The preamble to the treaty has the first legally binding acknowledgement of the division of what is now the European Union into regions. The preamble includes:

> Anxious to strengthen the unity of their economies and to ensure their harmonious development by reducing the differences existing between the various regions and backwardness of the less favoured regions

While this may seem to be an aspiration only, vague and undefined, preambles in Continental and now EU law are not as they are in British law, merely an introduction of little legal consequence. Instead preambles are legally binding and define how subsequent articles should be interpreted.

Furthermore, this clause of the preamble has to be taken in

the context of the whole preamble of eight points, which leads with

> Determined to lay the foundations of an ever-closer union among the people of Europe

Taking the two clauses together leaves little doubt that the long term aim of the 1957 treaty, which six countries signed, was one united country divided into regions.[1]

In the 1960s while the UK was trying to join the EEC, British academics discussed this issue of an EEC regional policy. One article published in 1967 came to the conclusion that clauses in the treaty of Rome equated to a defined regional policy.[2] Although the treaty did not precisely define what was meant by a common regional policy, in contrast for example with its more substantive clauses on transport and agriculture, yet all EEC functions were written in terms of regions.

For example,

○ article 39 (2a) on agriculture reads 'account shall be taken of the particular nature of agricultural activity, which results from . . . structural and natural disparities between the various regions'

○ article 49 (d) on the employment market requires the avoidance of 'serious threats to the standard of living and level of employment in the various regions and industries'

○ article 80 (2) on transport where 'the Commission shall . . . tak(e) account of in particular of the requirements of an appropriate regional economic policy.'[3]

In 1957 there was no precise geographical definition of regions. That was to come later.

Brussels defines

So regions and regional economic government were a legal component of the EEC from its beginning. And it did not take too long for the European Commission to develop them and give them a definition that was lacking in the treaty of Rome.

Four years later in 1961, the Commission held its first conference in Brussels on regional economies.

The Commission took its authority to hold the conference not only from the treaty of Rome, but also from its own paid advisory groups. The *unelected* Economic and Social Committee (ECOSOC) of the EEC referred a resolution to the *unelected* European Parliament proposing that a triumvirate of the Commission, national governments and regional authorities should develop regional policies.[4]

Endorsed by this notional authority, the Commission set up three committees in 1964 to investigate how existing regional government operated in the member states, and ways and means to run a regional policy in the EEC. In 1965 these reports formed part of the 120-page *First Commission Communication on Regional Policy* published in French.[5]

Again, the Commission expressly took its authority over the regions of member states from the treaty of Rome, in particular citing the preamble, article 2 on the promotion of 'a harmonious development of economic activities . . . throughout the Community', and more articles from the treaty.[6]

Addressing the practical problems of organising a regional policy, the Commission emphasised the importance of the regular meetings of national senior civil servants in Brussels to co-ordinate policy.[7]

The Commission stated in its conclusion to the Communication that

○ every member state must draw up regional economic

policies. The regions were defined as areas forming a coherent social and economic unit.

o Governments were to set up regional economic and social studies with an emphasis on the poorer industrial and agricultural areas.

o these studies were to form the basis for EEC grants, particularly from the European Investment Bank (EIB) in Luxembourg, itself set up under the treaty of Rome to develop 'the common market in the interest of the community.'[8]

To oversee all this, in 1968 the Commission set up a Regional Policy Directorate, now called DG XVI. Its mission to 'strengthen economic, social and territorial cohesion by reducing disparities between the levels of development of regions and countries of the European Union' enables the Commission using its structural funds to intervene and interfere in any part of the EU and to an extent in any country applying to join.

A four pronged attack

Regionalisation of the EEC (now the EU) has been driven from four directions: the Commission, national civil servants, Eurostat, and Brussels' grants.

First, the Commission, the legal overseer and instigator, took expert advice; it ensured exchanges of view between national civil servants responsible for regional policy, the European Investment Bank and the regions; it co-ordinated policies between member countries on state aid and transport; and improved transport between what it calls the outer and central regions of the EEC.

Secondly, and virtually unnoticed, working parties of senior civil servants, responsible for regional economic policy from member states, have advised both their own governments and the Commission.

Thirdly, Eurostat, the EU's statistical department in Luxembourg, has been crucial. The First Community Economic Programme of 1966 to 1970 was based on regions, and Eurostat was charged with creating uniform regions and improving regional statistics. The programme emphasised building transport routes across Europe and grants for poorer regions.

That neatly brought in the fourth essential element of grants, Brussels' bribes in all but name, to guarantee that authorities, both national and local, behaved in the approved Brussels' fashion.

Commission bribery

In 1958, the European Investment Bank (EIB), the EEC's financing institution, was set up. Through it, the EEC began to give grants and loans and soon added its 'structural funds' to ensure that all member countries would change their systems of government to receive crumbs from the Brussels' table.

One of the world's least known yet largest financial institutions, in 2003 the EIB approved even more loans than the World Bank worth £31.3 billion (or $58 bn). The Bank reveals little information about one third of its lending, called global loans.

Owned by the Member States, the EIB raises its funds on the capital markets and works closely with the EU Commission by what it terms 'enhanced co-operation' and describes its task as the EU's financing institution

> 'to contribute towards the integration, balanced development and economic and social cohesion of the Member Countries.'[9]

The Bank's interpretation of this is broad: it loans money to projects as diverse as the Brussels' public transport system, the light metro network in Tunis, a liquefied natural gas plant in Egypt, a power plant in Thailand, and a ring road in Amman, Jordan. It obviously believes in spreading the EU's influence very far and very wide.

The five EU structural funds are more narrowly directed with the overt intent of helping underdeveloped regions, in particular those with fading traditional industries, and combating long-term unemployment.

The European Social Fund, set up in 1960, is the main instrument of EU social policy to promote mobility of labour, and gives grants for retraining, resettlement costs and job creation schemes.

The European Regional Development Fund (ERDF) was agreed at the Heads of Government meeting in October 1973 to target the most disadvantaged EEC regions. At the time it was regarded as a diplomatic triumph for the British Prime Minister, Edward Heath.[10] At the least it would claw back some of Britain's contribution to the Common Agricultural Fund. On top of that, the British government insisted that it came into operation in 1974 at the same time as the proposed second stage of Economic and Monetary Union (EMU) intended to lead to a single currency, to lessen any bad publicity prompted by the convergence criteria. That attempt at EMU failed because of oil price shocks followed by world recession.

The ERDF promotes 'economic and social cohesion' 'by reducing inequalities between regions or social groups'. The money goes to EU-approved small businesses and local projects. Between 2000 and 2006 over £80 billion (or $148 bn) in grants is being paid to regions or sub regions lagging behind the EU regional average. In Britain those regions are South Yorkshire, West Wales and The Valleys, Cornwall and the Scilly Isles, Merseyside, the Peace Programme in Northern Ireland and the Border Regions of Ireland.

The other three structural funds are: the European Agricultural Guidance and Guarantee Fund to promote the Common Agricultural Policy; the Financial Instrument for Fisheries Guidance 'to increase competitiveness in the fishing industry, while . . . balancing fishing capacity and available resources'; and the Cohesion Fund for the most deprived countries of the EU, currently but not for long, Ireland, Portugal, Spain and Greece.[11]

Nations be damned

In 1969, the Commission produced a second and more substantial declaration on regional policy, *Une politique régionale pour la Communauté*.[12] Throughout its 240 pages the Commission determinedly undermined the independence of the nation states.

The Commission stated that

- ○ the EEC or the regions were to determine all economic and social policy *and not* the nation states
- ○ if member states remained responsible for regional policy then the development of the EEC would be jeopardised: 'harmonious economic development' could not be left to the member states[13]
- ○ only the Community could count the economic and social cost of public policies
- ○ only the Commission could offset the tendency of businesses to gravitate to the most developed part of the EEC
- ○ emphasis was again given to the European Investment Bank and member states *had* to assist investment by the Bank in their regions.

The Commission proposed a programme that it would lead

and control, and which in time would dramatically shift power from the member countries to the Commission:

1 The Commission will supervise, allocate priorities, and review with each country every year all regional development plans emphasising regions with agriculture, declining industries, and the critical regions adjacent to national borders.

2 The Commission reserves the right to ensure development plans will be undertaken in specified regions.

3 Regional Development plans must analyse all economic aspects; give a proposed action plan with dates and detail public and private financing.

4 The Commission will examine each state's development plan in the interests of the Common Market and steadily merge their economic policies.

5 The Commission emphasises the importance of improving the co-ordination of Member states' measures especially in border regions; the needs of the Community in managing infrastructure especially communications, oil, gas, ports, airports, and natural resources; the implications of agricultural policy; the need for a Community industrial policy.

6 The Commission will review instances of State aid.

7 The Commission will allocate Regional Development Fund monies.

8 The Commission will set up a permanent committee for regional development with representatives from member states and chaired by a member of the Commission. The EIB will send an observer. The Commission will agree its rules. The Committee will examine all Member States regional development plans and all regional policies of the Common Market.

9 The Commission will review with each State the impact
of these plans in the medium term.

10 Further instructions will be developed as necessary.[14]

This draconian policy directly attacked the proper preserves
of sovereign states. Regions were interlinked across national
borders with neighbouring regions, thus challenging those
national borders.

The Commission stressed its own dominant role in all infrastructure projects including oil, gas, ports, airports and
natural resources.

The Commission emphasised joint financing of public and
private funds that has been such a feature of all EU and EU-
related projects, thus drawing not only governments but also
private industry into its projects. As the declaration proposed,
joint public and private financing now dominates EU capital
projects.

What remained unfinished business were the geographical
borders of regions. Regions at that time were described only in
economic terms as industrialised, semi-industrialised and agricultural regions.

So it is certain that when Britain signed the treaty of Rome
in 1972, regional economic government was part of the *acquis
communautaire* binding on all applicant countries. (The *acquis*
comprises the treaties, regulations and directives passed by the
European institutions and all judgements of the European
Court of Justice.)

At the time only a few people close to the issue realised these
implications of the treaty of Rome.

Several decades later it is becoming clear that regions are the
EU's local government. Indeed, as we shall see, all the countries of the enlarged EU are now divided into regions, sub
regions and sub sub regions; some are encouraged to speak
languages which fell by the linguistic wayside centuries ago;

interlinked by roads, railways, cables and pipelines that ensure dependency on neighbouring regions and deliberately cut across national borders, with the intent to destroy them.

CHAPTER 3

Regionalising Britain is a Long Term Project

When Britain was Britain still

Over the centuries, substantive change to British local government has been rare. The last major milestone was the 1835 Municipal Corporations Act, which established directly elected corporate boroughs to replace the often corrupt and discredited self-electing mediaeval corporations. That Act was copied in Australia, New Zealand, Canada, India and parts of Africa.

After 1835 local government was democratic, low cost and generally effective. First-past-the-post voting, the secret ballot and the equality of councillors ensured a high degree of independence, transparency and honesty.[1]

Yet that should not imply a picture of contentment. By 1900 it was true that British local government was satisfactorily divided into county councils, county boroughs, districts and villages. Most of the problems, which had bedevilled local government in the nineteenth century, were resolved. But conflict quickly resurfaced over the role of education authorities. It continued with the administration of the Poor Law, which was eventually broken up by the Beveridge report[2] and subsequent Acts, notably the creation of the National Health Service in 1946. Ever rising costs made the rate support grant a major item of public expenditure and of public disquiet.

Above all, as the population expanded so the need to change boundaries increased, requiring both a re-think of local government and of the services it provided.

There were no easy solutions. The 1946 to 1948 Commission to re-draw the local government map of England and Wales was dissolved without a single change to a single boundary. Stalemate proved to be the pattern for the next ten committees and more under both Conservative and Labour governments.[3]

There was a common tension throughout the plethora of committees and commissions: resistance to government attempts, piecemeal though they were, to centralise and standardise the provision of services and to increase efficiency; and local defence of the right to provide services as the local authority saw fit, at least up to a minimum standard within the law.

The battle was the perennial one of centralisation versus local independence and local democracy. That battle never extended much beyond those intimately involved in central and local government. It rarely became a popular issue.

But no one suggested that the answer to all these stresses and strains on local life should be a new division of the UK into regions and the abolition of counties.

In the regional foothills
It was only when the British government began overtures to join the EEC that regions appeared on any political agenda. So far it has taken over 30 years to manoeuvre the British to accept regional government required by Britain's membership of the EU.

In order to overcome that trenchant British resistance, changes to local government have been presented only as

British solutions to British problems. That is until Tony Blair, the Prime Minister, remarked in the House of Commons in November 2004, but without further explanation, that 'there had to be a regional dimension' to government.[4]

The first time regions appeared on a British map was in 1964, that is after Britain had first applied to join the EEC, had been rejected but was continuing to make overtures. By that time the EEC Commission had already begun to define its regional policy.

George Brown, in charge of the Department of Economic Affairs in Harold Wilson's Labour government and an ardent campaigner for Britain to join the EEC, set up eight economic planning boards and councils on a *regional* basis.[5] Brown's division of the UK into much larger units than ever before, with contrived boundaries, was not publicly linked to the EEC.

The new boards had a close resemblance to today's regional development agencies. Boards of civil servants were responsible to ministers, and councils of the representatives of local authorities, together with unelected representatives of business, unions, charities, arts and tourism.

Today they are termed 'stakeholders'.

The boards and councils proved short lived. Designed to operate within the Labour government's national plan for economic growth, the 1966 balance of payments crisis, which forced the government to cut expenditure, raise interest rates and impose an incomes freeze, ended the national plan and ended Regional Economic Planning Councils too.

Redcliffe-Maud's 'holocaust'

When President de Gaulle famously said 'Non' in 1963 he ended Prime Minister Harold Macmillan's hopes that Britain would join the EEC. Yet there remained a quiet assumption among many MPs and the civil service that despite de Gaulle

Britain would succeed. It was just a question of time. De Gaulle would not be president of France forever.

The Labour Government did not wait, however, for de Gaulle to leave the political stage but applied again in 1967. Again de Gaulle said 'Non'. George Brown, refusing to take no for an answer, kept Britain's application on the table backed by all three main political parties and profited from the resignation of de Gaulle in April 1969. The EEC then agreed that Britain could begin negotiations for membership.

Only one year after the EEC Commission promulgated its *First Commission Communication on Regional Policy*, part of the acquis communautaire, the British government set in train an overhaul of local government structure.

In May 1966 Richard Crossman, Labour's Minister of Housing and Local Government, set up the Redcliffe-Maud Royal Commission, which reported in 1969.[6] While part of Crossman's thinking may have been to fight George Brown's challenge to his own Ministry, a Whitehall turf war, it went much further.

Lord Redcliffe-Maud later proclaimed in the House of Lords that his report would cause 'a holocaust of local authorities . . . the primrose way to the everlasting bonfire.'[7] Never before had there been such a wide-ranging and substantial enquiry into local government. It proved to be a major turning point.

The 1969 Commission advocated a total overhaul of all local government, creating in the process much bigger units. It proposed regional government in England introducing a new tier of eight provincial councils. The councils would replace George Brown's Regional Economic Planning Councils and combine the regional organisations for further education, sports, the arts, and tourism.

Council members were to be *indirectly* elected from existing councils and the remainder co-opted from different walks of life, the 'stakeholders' again, with the remit 'to settle the provincial strategy and planning framework within which the main authorities will operate.' That is exactly what the regional assemblies do today.

Below the new provincial councils, the Commission wanted root and branch reform: the abolition of counties, county boroughs, boroughs, urban district and rural district councils. They would be replaced by a single tier of unitary authorities; indeed the word unitary first appeared in this report. For example, the division between town and country was no longer desirable or relevant and the two should be combined. Rural areas strenuously disputed that.

Heath's underhand revolution

Before the new system could be fully implemented, the 1970 General Election returned the Conservatives to power and Edward Heath to 10 Downing Street. For political reasons Heath had to be seen *not* to adopt all Labour's proposals, notably the regions: the Conservatives had campaigned on the slogan of 'two tiers everywhere'.[8] So the subsequent 1972 Local Government Act dropped provincial councils pending the report of the Royal Commission on the Constitution set up three years earlier (see page 38).

It was no coincidence that at the same time Heath was negotiating to take Britain into the EEC. In 1972 Heath signed the treaty of Rome, with its requirement for regional economic government to replace existing local government. This was given no publicity and it may be fair to assume that knowledge of it was limited to interested academics, civil servants and a few MPs.

Regions were certainly not part of the lengthy negotiation between the British government and the countries of the EEC. Nor were they mentioned later in the campaign for the 1975 referendum on whether or not the UK should stay in the EEC.

The only issue at the time was whether or not financial help to certain parts of the country, like Merseyside, could continue once the UK was inside the EEC. A *Sunday Times* article headed 'Six take tough line on UK regional aid' stirred the issue briefly, causing a small flurry of ministerial replies to anxious MPs.[9]

In London no one was openly suggesting that the EEC would have any role in regional planning, but Britain's chief negotiator Geoffrey Rippon MP acknowledged that in Brussels it was a current issue. He quoted Signor Altiero Spinelli, the EEC Commissioner for Industrial Affairs,

> 'this does not mean that regional planning should be completely run from Brussels. We think that the main initiative should remain with the national governments and local authorities.'[10]

The central platitude was contained in notes for Prime Minister's Questions in the House of Commons. If the question were asked 'why has not HMG raised regional policy questions in the negotiations', the proposed slippery answer was

> 'There has been nothing to discuss. The Community know of our regional problems and policies. There is no Community regional policy as such. If any question were to arise we could certainly broach it with the Community.'[11]

Heath attacks counties
Even though Heath put only part of the Redcliffe-Maud Commission's recommendations into operation, the result was still 'a holocaust of local authorities', just as Lord Redcliffe-Maud had predicted. In 1974 ancient cities and boroughs were swept away; urban districts and rural districts ceased to exist; aldermen were abolished; ancient charters and liberties,

traditions and privileges, courts of record and courts of hustings were all destroyed.

Although Heath's government failed to divide the country into regions, as the Redcliffe-Maud Commission had proposed, it did create the EEC's sub-regions, although not by that name. A new layer of unitary authorities or districts was introduced between the counties and the parishes: they incorporated existing boroughs, urban districts, and rural districts. County boroughs were merged into existing authorities. Parish councils were given slightly more powers (a watered down version of Redcliffe-Maud) but those powers were not extended to towns as previously intended.

Alarm and outrage accompanied this wholesale transformation of English boundaries, many of which had existed for hundreds of years. Changes to counties caused particular anger and even today Ted Heath is blamed for this assault on the county structure.

So great was the upheaval that the reaction was country-wide. No doubt if it had been realised that most of the changes were to satisfy Britain's proposed EEC membership the reaction would have been volcanic.

While many proposals were quickly thrown out, the government stood firm on the issue of changes to or abolition of county councils. At the time only the campaign to preserve the Isle of Wight succeeded, the government had wanted to merge it with Hampshire.

Three new counties were created from adjoining ones: Avon (from Somerset and Gloucestershire); Cleveland (from Durham and the North Riding of Yorkshire) and Humberside (from eastern Yorkshire).

Two new counties were formed from mergers: Cumbria (formerly Westmoreland and Cumberland) and Hereford and Worcester combined.

The county of Rutland was abolished, becoming merely a

district in Leicestershire. Huntingdonshire was merged into Cambridgeshire. Middlesex disappeared into Greater London. Yorkshire was divided into Humberside, North Yorkshire, and West Yorkshire.

Parts of the county of Surrey were first given to neighbouring authorities and then after a long fight returned.

Less contentious were the six new metropolitan counties, including Greater Manchester, recognising that it made sense to combine the city with outlying towns, but even then some proposed boundaries did not survive the initial furore. Greater Manchester lost some of its 'new' towns before it started and thirteen other smaller adjustments were made to county boundaries.

Revolution in the Celtic fringe

Northern Ireland went through a similar upheaval but a year earlier in 1973. All the counties, county borough, and districts were replaced. In their stead was a single tier of 26 district councils within what was the unspoken single region of Northern Ireland. All the old county names – Antrim, Armagh, Down, Fermanagh, Londonderry and Tyrone – remained as the names of district councils to satisfy local sensibilities.

In Wales the new counties of 1974 bore little or no relation to the old. Consigned to the dustbin of history were the counties of Breconshire, Caernarvonshire, Cardiganshire, Carmarthenshire, Denbighshire, Flintshire, Merionethshire, Monmouthshire, Montgomeryshire, Pembrokeshire and Radnorshire.

Thirteen counties were reduced to eight, with boundaries unknown to any previous generation. Glamorgan apart, all the new names were Welsh with no English equivalent, and taken from ancient Welsh kingdoms or even derived from Roman names. For example, Monmouthshire became Gwent, and the three counties of Cardiganshire, Pembrokeshire and

Carmarthenshire became the single county of Dyfed. The name Dyfed is derived from the Roman, Demetia.

In Scotland, the restructuring took place a year later than in England and Wales and was just as revolutionary. In 1975, at a stroke of the pen, and following the recommendations of yet another Royal Commission,[12] all 34 of Scotland's historic counties disappeared to be replaced by nine regions. Beneath them were 53 district councils.

Unlike Wales, the old and familiar Scottish county names drawing local allegiance continued. But the counties became unitary authorities within the new regions of Grampian, Tayside, Strathclyde, Highland, Borders, Dumfries and Galloway, Lothian, Central and Fife plus single tier authorities serving the Western Isles, Orkney and Shetland.

So Wales, Scotland and Northern Ireland now had regions and sub-regions, only England was stuck half way to the new Brussels' system.

In 1977 Harold Wilson, the Prime Minister, tried again but failed. He recommended a limited change of two pathfinder regional authorities: the North (to include what is now Cumbria) and Yorkshire and Humberside. They were seen then and now to be the most likely to accept regional authorities because of strong local loyalties, especially in Yorkshire.

CHAPTER 4

Who Masterminded the Regional Revolution?

A Trojan horse for regional government

So according to the treaty of Rome and later EEC Commission Decisions, a country wishing to be a member of the EEC would have to adopt the EEC's regional system. Chapter 3 laid out the major changes in Britain's local government after 1964 and pointed to Britain's courting of the EEC as the main reason.

What has yet to be explored is how these fundamental changes in the UK came about, and which caused such a public outcry. The quick answer is the British government, both Conservative and Labour. While that is of course true, there was also a campaign outside government to promote the division of the whole of the UK into regions.

In 1964, while the unelected EU Commission was developing its policy of regional government, an unofficial body called the Study of Parliament Group first met at the London School of Economics to review 'the problem of the effectiveness of Parliament as a whole'. It still meets today.

Its members are mainly academics with some civil servants who work in the Palace of Westminster. The Group expressly excludes MPs as members. Despite that, MPs do regularly take part in meetings and conferences and are influential in its direction.

At its beginning, one highly influential man with the group, though because he was an MP he could not be a member of it, was Richard Crossman. As Minister for of Housing and Local Government Crossman set up the Redcliffe-Maud Royal Commission and thus set in train that 'holocaust of local authorities'. He was also a prominent member of the Fabian Society.

This was no accident. The Study of Parliament Group is a Fabian front organisation and its agenda is revolutionary.[1] Its bland and unassuming title, worthy aims, mixed political membership and practical discussions enable it to exert significant influence.

The Fabian Society is at the cutting edge of socialism in Britain, and since the First World War has been at the heart of the drive for a federal Europe.[2] Most proposals and campaigns have emanated from its members, either directly or indirectly.[3]

G D H Cole, a Fabian historian and economist, wrote in 1943 that Fabians want 'British Socialism in the British tradition, rather than Russian Socialism.'[4] Cole's wife, Margaret, noted that

> 'Fabians appeared in so many desirable liberal (and cultural) connections that they could scarcely be believed to be subversive of private property or of liberty.'[5]

Therefore, dogmatism and violent revolution are out and reasonableness and tolerance are the projected qualities. While Fabians may join any political party, most are in the Labour Party. Since the 1997 general election there have been around 200 Fabian MPs in the House of Commons, amongst whom number nearly entire Labour Cabinets, including Tony Blair, Gordon Brown, Robin Cook, Jack Straw, David Blunkett,

Peter Hain, Patricia Hewitt, John Reid, Ruth Kelly, Alan Millburn and Clare Short.

The Fabian Society adapted the idea of front organisations, like the Study of Parliament Group, from the Soviet Union and the NKVD (the forerunner of the KGB). The first in Britain was Political and Economic Planning set up in 1934, and now called the Policy Studies Institute. Other well known groups include the Federal Trust and Charter 88. Amongst campaigning activities, they give evidence to Commissions, and to House of Lords Select Committees and interact at all levels of government.

This approach is both subtle and clever. The Fabian practice has always been to operate circles within circles, encourage divergent views, and deliberately muddy the waters. So these front organisations have predominantly non-Fabian membership, preferably as broad a mix as possible, but the direction comes from the Fabians.

In the case of the Study of Parliament Group, the two founders were Michael Ryle, a highly respected clerk in the House of Commons between 1951 and 1989, and Sir Bernard Crick, an academic of repute and a leading member of the Fabian Society. More recently Sir Bernard has launched the Association for Citizenship Teaching and chaired an advisory group to the Home Office on citizenship training in schools.[6] He was knighted in 2002 for 'services to citizenship in schools and to political studies.'

At its second conference in 1966 the Study of Parliament Group discussed a report on Regionalism in Parliament in a 'full and lively' fashion.[7] Subsequently an article called *Regionalism and Parliament* appeared in the *Political Quarterly* in 1967 a magazine edited by Bernard Crick.[8] This concluded that clauses in the Treaty of Rome equated to a defined regional policy (see page 16).

Kilbrandon reports

In 1969, just after the Redcliffe-Maud Commission reported, the Labour Government set up yet another investigation, the Royal Commission on the Constitution, known as the Kilbrandon Commission. That reported four years later.[9] If anything it was more radical than the Redcliffe-Maud Commission. Even its terms of reference sounded bizarre to British ears accustomed to a unified country for over 300 years: to examine the structures of UK government, its constituent nations and regions, and propose changes.

Various ways of devolving government functions from London to Scotland, to Wales and to the new English regions were considered, including dividing the UK into separate sovereign states. Over thirty years later 'the nations' is accepted government language: the Deputy Prime Minister chairs a Cabinet Committee on the Nations and Regions to review progress on 'Devolution'.

The Commission was set up, as it said, in response to dissatisfaction with the centralisation of government and administration, particularly in Scotland, Wales and the more economically depressed parts of England. Its remit was to discover the causes of the discontent and to lay down principles for reform.

The chief campaigner for the 'dissatisfaction', in particular the devolution of powers to Scotland and to a Scottish parliament, was the Labour MP and leading Fabian, Professor John P. Mackintosh. Mackintosh had been a founder member of the Study of Parliament Group but under its rules had to resign when he was elected to the House of Commons. Like his fellow MP Richard Crossman, he remained influential in the Group.

Many years later in a House of Lords debate on devolution, a former General Secretary of the Fabian Society, Lord

Rodgers of Quarry Bank, commented on Professor Mackintosh's influence,

> 'However, if we are to consider the progenitors of what we are discussing today, I should like to pay tribute to the late John Mackintosh, who was then a Labour Member of Parliament.[10] His book on the devolution of power, published in 1968, was not only a significant contribution to what later took place in Scotland in particular, as well as in Wales, but also set out a blueprint of a kind for the form of English regionalism that we are discussing today.'[11]

A majority on the Kilbrandon Commission favoured regional councils, part elected and part appointed, but that plan was rejected as too bureaucratic and expensive. Yet despite its overwhelming shortcomings, this plan is the one adopted today.

The Commission maintained that

> 'momentous as entry into Europe is, it does not have any major specific consequences for the questions remitted to us. In particular, it does not rule out devolution.'

This relied on the argument that the powers, which the Kilbrandon Commission proposed should be devolved, coincided only to a limited extent with the powers within the EEC's responsibility.

The dissenters

Not every member of the Commission shared that view. Lord Crowther-Hunt and Professor Alan Peacock argued in a *memorandum of dissent* that EEC membership 'imposes serious constraints on the form and extent of any system of devolution'. They noted that the EEC's responsibilities were evolving and that a range of responsibilities and objectives had been identified at the 1972 Paris Summit with far-reaching ramifications for the debate on domestic constitutional change.

The dissenters listed six ways in which EEC membership might affect British governance. It would

○ remove important areas of decision making still further from the British people
○ strengthen the bureaucracy
○ make it imperative that Parliament should become an effective countervailing force
○ increase the load on central government machinery
○ strengthen any case there may be for devolution of some responsibilities of Whitehall and Westminster to subordinate units of government within the UK
○ simultaneously provide serious constraints on the form and extent of devolution that might be devised.

They argued that it would be unwise to devolve legislative power in any area where that power was moving to Brussels,

> 'If legislative power were to be given to the government of any 'nation or region' within the United Kingdom on any matter that might be the subject of policy making in Brussels, there is no provision in the Treaty of Rome and the Treaty of Accession for that government to be separately represented in Brussels on either the Council of Ministers or the Committee of Permanent Representatives when the matter is being discussed or decided. Nor is it at all likely that the United Kingdom could secure such a concession. Thus, we should have the spectacle of policy being made in an area for which a subordinate government in theory had full responsibility, but was excluded from the forum which takes all the main decisions.'

Finally, they noted that the 'ambit of Brussels is so potentially all-embracing' that this left 'very little scope for real legislative devolution'.
The two dissenters have proved to be right.

Devolution: the end of Britain?

Plans for devolution were proposed in White Papers in 1975 and 1976, but were eventually reduced to referendums on the issue in Scotland and Wales.[12] A Scottish Parliament had last met in Edinburgh on 25th March 1707. Wales had in practice been united with England since 1284.

The main pressure came from the Scottish National Party and Plaid Cymru (the Party of Wales), which between them had won 14 seats at the 1974 election. The Labour Government was vulnerable, because by 1977 its majority had been whittled down to zero by successive by-election defeats.

A terrific battle ensued in the House of Commons when the Labour government introduced a combined Scotland and Welsh Bill to put the Kilbrandon Commission's recommendations into effect. It only gained a second reading when the Government conceded referendums to gauge the popular will. The Shadow Secretary of State for Scotland, Alick Buchanan-Smith and Malcolm Rifkind, a Conservative spokesmen for Scotland, resigned when their party opposed the second reading. After more than 100 hours of debate on amendments, the Bill was withdrawn.

22 Labour MPs defied their party's whip on this issue of central importance. Their leader, the Scottish Labour MP Tam Dalyell, wrote

> 'to suggest that England, Scotland and Wales might once again be parted from one another has always seemed absurd, impractical and entirely undesirable.'

He strongly advocated building

'on *existing* instructions rather than burden the country with an impractical and expensive additional layer of government, the political implications of which would be far more wide-ranging and disruptive than well intentioned devolutionists care to imagine.'[13]

Dalyell, a fiercely independent and outspoken MP, argued that a Scottish assembly financially dependent on the UK Government would be in an impossible position. And trying to separate specifically Scottish issues from those affecting the UK as a whole would be nigh impossible. Therefore, the very existence of the assembly would lead to conflict with London and to demands for a break with the UK. The title of his book *Devolution: The End of Britain?* summed up his position.

In late 1977 the Labour government tried again with two separate Bills for Scotland and Wales. This time they succeeded because those who had opposed the combined Bill on the grounds that the Welsh did not really want a separate Assembly were mollified. In committee an amendment was forced on the government to repeal the Acts unless 40 per cent of the whole electorate voted Yes.

In 1979 the Prime Minister, James Callaghan, duly held the referendums for assemblies in Scotland and Wales. They failed at the ballot box. The required threshold of electors voting was not met. In Scotland, only 32.5 per cent bothered to vote, with only a small majority in favour.[14] In Wales, a large majority voted against.

CHAPTER 5

The UK is Broken Up

John Major straddles the divide

Regions were conspicuous by their absence during Mrs. Thatcher's three governments. But her Conservative governments were responsible for transferring more power from local government to central government with rate capping, and the payment of business property rates direct to the Treasury. Thus she deprived locally elected councillors of discretion to provide local services and on which the voters could judge them. Tinkering with local taxation culminated in the hated Poll Tax and riots on London's streets.

This was all done in the name of efficiency and fiscal probity but it did nothing to promote local democracy, quite the reverse was true. The only thing that can be said is that it had nothing to do with the EU. Unfortunately Mrs Thatcher's policies also gave a strong argument to those who later promoted regional government, Britain had indeed become highly centralised.

Regions resurfaced under her successor, John Major.[1] In 1994 Major's Conservative government, in which scepticism of the European project was driven to the wastelands of political thought, established Government Offices for the Regions,

UK in regions

outposts of central government civil servants to deliver government policy.

On the one hand, Major curried popular favour by reverting to some pre-1974 boundaries; on the other hand he advanced the EU cause by creating Government Offices in the regions, regions which had not previously existed, and by extending unitary or sub-regional government, a pre-requisite of full regional government.

In 1995, picking up where Harold Wilson had left off, the first Regional Assembly for Yorkshire and Humberside was established combining the Regional Planning Office, the Yorkshire and Humberside Regional Association and its Brussels' office in an area of 22 local authorities.[2]

Perhaps paradoxically it was Major's government which reversed some of the most hated of Ted Heath's changes. In particular in 1996 the eight huge Welsh counties with their 37 districts councils were abolished and replaced by 22 unitary authorities. Simultaneously, in Scotland the nine regions, the three island authorities and 53 district councils set up in 1975[3] were replaced by 32 unitary authorities.

Today, it is clear that Scotland, Wales and Northern Ireland are regions in their own right, that the Heath regional divisions do not fit Brussels' current regulations.

In England the changes were more varied and the pattern of local government reverted to something similar to the pre-1974 holocaust. The changes were phased to take effect on 1st April in each year between 1995 and 1998.

In particular in 1996 four of Heath's hated counties – Avon, Cleveland, Humberside and the combined Hereford and Worcester – were all abolished and converted into numbers of unitary authorities plus Worcestershire County Council. The people of Rutland who had fought hard for thirty years to have their county restored were satisfied by the compromise of a unitary authority called Rutland.

In 1998, the Royal County of Berkshire ceased to exist, its Royal status abolished and now it only exists for ceremonial functions. The Lord Lieutenant and the High Sheriff remain: the substance of government has gone. Berkshire is in six unitary authorities.

Labour promotes regions

While in opposition, the Labour Party remained committed to regional government: it featured in both the 1992 and 1997 Party manifestos. A 1995 consultation paper, *A Choice for England*, proposed indirectly elected regional chambers and ultimately regional assemblies. London would have an elected strategic authority combining both city and regional functions.[4]

In marked contrast to its position today, the Labour Party had no problem admitting a Brussels' connection with regional government. It stated,

> 'Labour wants to transfer power to the local level and encourage Scotland, Wales and Northern Ireland and the regions of England to strengthen their links with the rest of Europe to allow them to influence the decision making process in Brussels and benefit more from European regional and structural policy.'[5]

On gaining office, the Labour government under Prime Minister Tony Blair acted almost at once. In July 1997 it published White Papers proposing a Scottish Parliament and a National Assembly for Wales, and rushed to a referendum in September.[6] With the summer holidays intervening, there was no time for a serious debate.

In Scotland, 74.3 per cent voted for a Scottish Parliament.

The Labour government's enthusiasm for this socialist revolution is imprinted in its 'Policy Documents' and 'Guidance' on local government published since 1997.[7] There have been over

100 of them, more than one new publication for every month Labour has been in power, with well-worn socialist titles like 'New Deal'.[8]

It is time to worry about one-man one vote, when the government writes of 'removing the democratic deficit'.[9] The Labour government's intent to superimpose an elected regional assembly was an answer to what John Prescott recognised were undemocratic quangos and 'strategic partnerships' – over 60 quangos and 140 partnerships in each region of England alone. But he had no intention of abolishing them. [10]

Was the Welsh referendum biased?

In Wales the referendum result was extremely close: the Yes vote won by a margin of only 6,721 votes. 50.3 per cent voted Yes, and 49.7 per cent voted No.

Unlike Scotland where 45 per cent of the total electorate went to the polls, in Wales the total voting failed to reach that 40 per cent threshold required in 1979 for the result to count. The Blair government had such a large majority in the Commons that it could ignore the threshold issue, which had been forced on Callaghan's weak government.

Only a quarter of the Welsh electorate voted for a National Assembly for Wales and in Monmouthshire the figure was as low as 16 per cent. It was scarcely a resounding endorsement.

That is the moral case against the referendum. But it was worse than that.

The Committee on Standards in Public Life, set up by John Major with a wide ranging brief 'to act as . . . an ethical workshop called in to do running repairs',[11] reported in 1998

'We were disturbed, in particular, by the evidence we heard in Cardiff to the effect that the referendum campaign in Wales . . . was very one sided, with the last minute No organisation seriously under-funded and having to rely for financial support essentially on a single wealthy donor. The outcome of the Welsh referendum was extremely close, and a fairer campaign might well have resulted in a different outcome.'[12]

There appears to have been some deliberate manipulation of the No campaign.

○ That old political trick of 'bouncing' voters into voting Yes was used: the Welsh referendum was timed to be immediately after that for Scotland, where the Yes vote was expected to win easily, as indeed it did.

○ Derek Gregory of UNISON, the public services trade union, funded a massive Yes campaign across Wales and used UNISON facilities, without asking his members' permission.

○ There was no attempt to give equal broadcasting time to both campaigns. That was especially true of the BBC (financed by the general public) and *The Western Mail*, the largest circulation newspaper in Wales. Both favoured the Yes campaign.

○ Some suspected that No votes failed to reach the count. The No campaign was not present at the opening of postal votes. In Flintshire 6,000 No votes were reportedly missing. At the Rhondda Cynon Taff count, Labour supporters emptied ballot boxes behind a curtain, crudely sorted the ballot papers and then produced them from behind the curtain to the counters.

○ The count in Carmarthen was held up because of the late arrival of ballot boxes stuffed to the brim, in marked contrast to the other ballot boxes.

○ The No campaign presented fully audited accounts showing that 90 percent of its approximate £115,000 ($200,000) expenditure was by the banker, Sir Robert

Hodge. The government's Yes campaign, spending tax-payers' money, failed to produce any meaningful accounts. Sir Robert told the Neill Committee that 'I am led to believe that the other side . . . possibly spent a seven figure sum. That puts it in proportion.'[13]

Regional Development Agencies at home and abroad

With the quick success of the Scottish and Welsh referendums behind it, in 1998 the Labour Government established nine Regional Development Agencies (RDAs), one in each English region, including one in London based in St Katherine's Dock.[14] All these RDAs have a close working relationship with the civil servants in the neighbouring Government Offices (GOs).

The nine agencies are expensive to run costing over £1.8 billion a year ($3.2 bn); the most expensive is the North West Development Agency with a government allocation of £400 million a year ($720 m). They each employ between 100 and 350 staff.

At a cost of about £600 million a year ($1.08 bn) the Scottish Enterprise's role is to be a very expensive 'gateway' for EU grants.[15] With the Scottish Executive it runs a separate organisation, Scottish Development International. That has 21 small offices round the world and larger ones in Boston, Houston, San Jose, Shanghai and Singapore.

The Welsh Development Agency, sponsored by 'the Welsh Assembly government', has offices in Australia, Ottawa, Toronto, Beijing, Shanghai, France, Holland, Hong Kong, India, Ireland, Italy, Japan, Korea, Taiwan, London, California, Illinois and New York. All these are additional to the 'embassies' the Welsh First Minister is setting up (see page 93).

The largest agency is Invest Northern Ireland with 710 staff and an undisclosed budget.

The English RDAs are public bodies responsible to the Department for Trade and Industry in London; the government appoints 15 board members to each one.

The RDAs 'agreed' in 1999 to launch the eight 'English' regional assemblies, though as government bodies they were unlikely to refuse. Assembly members are not elected, they too are appointed. Each RDA consults with its regional assembly on the development of its Regional Economic Strategy, described as the 'route map' for each region's development.

In practice the staffs of the GOs, the RDAs and the regional assemblies are closely intertwined. Sharp-eyed watchers have spotted that some people have titles from each organisation and even muddle them on correspondence, using more than one at the same time.

The RDAs co-ordinate land use, transport, economic development, agriculture, energy and waste. Every RDA has a fully staffed office in Brussels and a close working relationship with the EU Commission.

They promote the regions as though they were a country. For example, the East of England Development Agency says it exports more to Europe than to the USA. Teams of businessmen go abroad touting the claims of each region for inward investment.

Two English RDAs have overseas offices. The North of England, in addition to its three offices in the Northeast and another in Brussels, has offices in Chicago, Atlanta, Boston, Los Angles, China, Korea, Taiwan and Tokyo.

The South East of England Development Agency (SEEDA) has offices in Washington, San Diego and Boston, Sidney, and two offices in Japan, in Yokohama and Osaka.

These must duplicate the work of the Department of Trade and Industry, which maintains a large number of offices round the world to promote British trade and are therefore an added and questionable heavy cost for the taxpayer.

London demoted to a regional capital

As a result of the steady break up of the UK, the London of the last 1,000 years will be no more. London will return to a regional capital, to the role it had before the twelfth century.

London now has a form of regional assembly, following the endorsement of less than a quarter of the electorate in a 1998 referendum.[16] Only 34 per cent of Londoners voted of whom just over 70 per cent said Yes.

This was even fewer than voted for a National Assembly for Wales. While in Wales questions about the legitimacy of its Assembly rumble on, Londoners have submitted without a murmur.

The Labour government has described the Greater London Assembly as a half way house to a regional assembly and that more changes are likely. John Prescott told the House of Commons that he had 'no doubt that reform will continue. As the Prime Minister reminds us constantly, change, change, change is always on the agenda.'[17]

The government has not yet made the nature of those changes public.

Just like the other English regions, the mushrooming of organisations and the criss-cross responsibilities between the various groups of people elected in London has made a farce of transparency and accountability. On top of that the London Assembly constituencies are so vast that there is only the most tenuous of constituency links. Nearly half of the Assembly members are not linked to a constituency at all.

Will there always be an England?

England's final destruction into nine parts began with the 2002 White Paper *Your Region, Your Choice* published in 2002.[18]

Reading the White Paper is an exercise in Kreminology: it abounds in obfuscations, deceptions and deceits. For example, the overused word partnership has no precise meaning. 'When

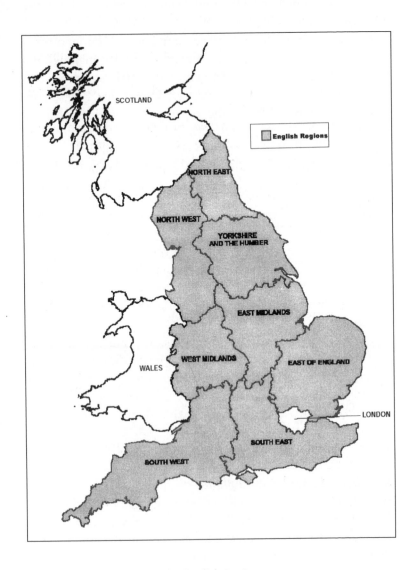

The English Regions

I use a word . . . it means just what I chose it to mean – neither more nor less' as Humpty Dumpty remarked in *Alice Through The Looking Glass*.[19]

The document is unimpressive: verbiage – 'economic cohesion', 'joined up government', 'joined up policy making' and 'joined up decisions' – is mixed with self-evident truths – 'plans have to be forward looking' and 'real knowledge' – with contradictions, dubious logic, and repetition. A wielder of a red pen could cut the paper in half and still have plenty of nonsense left over.

Your Region, Your Choice sheds a little light on the source of regional government. Through the verbal murk, the origin of words gives some of the game away. It is clear that the British White Paper is not wholly British. 'Spatial planning' is imported from France via Brussels and was unknown to British planners. 'Observatories', another EU favourite term, is derived from the French. The West Midlands region is to have a 'concordat' with other British government organisations.[20]

The government's repeated use of the word devolution is misleading. As already described, devolution is nothing new; all British local government has been devolved (see page 14).

Devolution disguises a three-stage process of revolution. First, some government offices are moved from London to the new regions. Second, some powers are taken from county councils and districts and given to regions, and third, the county councils are abolished or turned into unitary authorities, like Rutland.

The government avoids admitting that county councils are to be abolished and omits to say that regional government is required by treaty obligation to the EU.

The White Paper explicitly calls British local authorities subregions.[21] In a convoluted way it states,

'in any region where an elected Assembly is

53

established, there should be an associated move to a wholly unitary local government structure.'[22]

Those who favour an English parliament to match and counter-balance those in Scotland, Wales and Northern Ireland are answered elliptically. The White Paper notes that 84 per cent of the population of the UK lives in England. In a leap of logic it continues that there cannot therefore be an English parliament. Why not?

To satisfy logic, the White Paper should admit – but does not – that the population of England dominates the UK so an English parliament would also be dominant.

To achieve that EU revolution, England has to be broken up so that it cannot dominate. That is the White Paper's unwritten, but logical conclusion.

What the White Paper fails to say is that the ultimate 'devolution' will be from Brussels, because the powers given to regions are those powers that have already passed to Brussels.

Direct links to the EU in Brussels can be discovered elsewhere for those who care to dig, but those links are certainly not headlines. For example, the self-declared role of one directorate of the North West Regional Assembly is

> 'To progress the European agenda through the provision of a coherent and co-ordinated management infrastructure, the delivery and development of a range of EU funded programmes, building on existing partners arrangements with candidate countries, and the production of a regional European strategy.'[23]

The Assembly of European Regions (AER), with its logo of the EU ring of stars and declared aim of 'bringing together the regions of Europe and allowing them, together, to act in the construction of Europe and European integration', truthfully reported that 'it is a matter of fact that today about two thirds of all EU legislation and programmes are applied at the regional, or local level.'[24]

New capital cities add cost

If and when formally elected, the regional assemblies will decide on their capital cities. Where might they be? No doubt that will be strenuously debated. This list shows regional cities whose importance is already rising:

Region	Government Office	RDA HQ	Assembly HQ
SE	Guildford	Guildford	Guildford
SW	Bristol	Exeter	Taunton
NE	Newcastle	Newcastle	Newcastle
NW	Manchester	Liverpool	Wigan
Yorks/Humber	Leeds	Wakefield	Wakefield
W Midlands	Birmingham	Birmingham	Birmingham
E Midlands	Nottingham	Nottingham	Melton Mowbray
East of England	Cambridge	Bury St Edmunds	Bury St Edmunds

At present, most regional assemblies peregrinate around the region for their meetings like a mediaeval court. If regional capitals are chosen will the assemblies then demand new 'parliament' buildings like those for London, Scotland and Wales and at the cost of millions of pounds to the taxpayer? The answer is almost certainly yes.

Overseas Territories caught in the EU net

In 2001 the Overseas Territories qualified for EU grants. It stretches credulity that this is an entirely philanthropic exercise on the part of the EU. Grants given to constituent parts of all member countries have all had substantial strings attached, intended to lead to one unified country.

To help them through the commando course of paperwork, the Foreign and Colonial Office in 2003 appointed a EU-UK co-ordinator and money is now flowing to Anguilla, Monsterrat, Pitcairn, St Helena, the Turks and Caicos, and the Falklands. In 2004 they obtained financing worth overall €41 million. The Cayman Islands and the British Virgin Islands have outstanding bids.

Without a doubt, this EU funding will be at the price of some or all of the islands' freedom. They are already under EU attack as tax havens. The 2005 FCO Departmental Report referred to EU financing to promote integration and improve their partnership with the EU.

The story so far

Three elected regional governments have started work after referendums on their existence: London, Scotland and Wales. The Northern Ireland Assembly is in cold storage awaiting warmer political climes. It was suspended on 14th October 2002 when the peace process broke down, though elections were held a year later.

The remaining eight English regional assemblies are operating unelected, without democratic legitimacy. All these regional governments began work without considering the issue of elections and before the relevant act of parliament was passed or even drafted.

Worse, the eight referendums still pending in England are not to decide if there should be regional assemblies, but *only* if they should be elected assemblies. If the vote is No, the Assemblies will continue to operate unelected, just like the North East of England.

All the parliaments and assemblies are closely intertwined with developments agencies at home and abroad and government offices full of civil servants.

CHAPTER 6

Churchmen and Charities Campaign for Regions

Unlikely backers

'Campaign organisations have been established in a number of regions', the British government baldly declared in its 2002 White Paper, *Your Region, Your Choice*. For what were these organisations to campaign? The White Paper was silent.

These campaigns endorse regional government. Just like the campaigns in Scotland, Wales and London, they are one sided and funded with millions of pounds from the taxpayer, without the taxpayers' permission.

So the British government is deliberately obfuscating and the evidence suggests that the dice are heavily loaded in favour of the Yes vote, which the government wants.

Nor is it just taxpayers' money funding the campaigns. Charities have given money for a Yes vote. Yet the Charity Commission for England and Wales makes clear that an institution whose stated purposes include the achievement of a political purpose cannot be a charity.

Even more bizarre, bishops of the Church of England have led every Yes campaign.

There is no government money to promote the No argument, to oppose regional government, except the minimum required by law for the campaign itself just prior to a referendum. Private individuals have organised on a limited basis, but like the referendum campaign for the National Assembly for Wales they will be outspent and outplayed many times over by their own government, spending their own money.

Neil Herron, the Campaign Director of the North East Against Regional Assemblies, filed an official complaint with the Audit Commission. He alleged that Sunderland Council misused taxpayers' money. The Council, he said, had contributed over £92,000 ($170,000) for the year 2002-3 which was used by a third party to run publicity campaigns in favour of elected assemblies and that was in breach of the Code of Practice on Local Authority Publicity. The Audit Commission said 'guilty'.

That must be the tip of a very large iceberg.

Archbishops, Bishops and the Constitutional Conventions

The ways in which the British taxpayer has *involuntarily* funded the Yes campaigns for elected regional assemblies raise very serious questions.

The government established and the taxpayer funded Constitutional Conventions in six of England's eight regions to promote elected assemblies. The Conventions are run from either regional or local government buildings, which represent a further hidden subsidy.

It is no coincidence that the name used is the same as the Constitutional Convention, which designed the EU Constitution. Use of language can be most revealing as the 2002 White Paper, *Your Region, Your Choice* also showed.

They are organised on the same lines as the pioneer Constitutional Convention in Scotland in advance of its referendum. That group was partly funded by a charity, the Joseph Rowntree Reform Trust.[1]

Canon Kenyon Wright, then General Secretary of the

Scottish Churches Council, led the Scottish Constitutional Convention for ten years until the 1999 referendum returned a Yes vote for a Scottish Parliament. Wright claimed that two principles underlie the Scottish Parliament: 'citizens not subjects' and 'subsidiarity'.[2] He wrote

'The Convention, which included the broadest cross-section of Scottish society, worked by a new type of consensus-building, to put in place by 1995 "Scotland's Parliament; Scotland's Right" – a detailed proposal for a parliament that would be "radically different from the rituals of Westminster"'.[3]

Since retiring from the Church, Canon Wright has repeatedly stood for election for the Liberal Democrats in Scotland.

Bishops of the Church of England have chaired all the English Conventions, led by the Bishop of Durham, the Rt. Revd. Michael Turnbull for the North East. The Bishop of Liverpool has led the North West; the Bishop of Birmingham the West Midlands; the Bishop of St Albans the East of England, and the Bishop of Exeter the Southwest.

Most surprisingly of all, the Archbishop of York is president of the Campaign for Yorkshire.

The Labour government's use of the episcopal office for overt political campaigns is highly questionable, has provoked strong debate and yet continues unchecked.

Two regions have not had Constitutional Conventions, London and the South East. Could this be because the Archbishop of Canterbury (then the Most Revd. George Carey) and the Bishop of London (the Rt. Revd Richard Chartres) were not willing to head them?

The EU Commission makes a fleeting appearance

The Bishop of Exeter chaired the first South West Constitutional Convention held at Exeter University in May 2001. Also on the platform was Stefeen De Rynck, a Belgian from the Governance Team in the unelected European Commission in Brussels. He spelt out in impeccable English that holding the Convention was exactly what the EU Commission wished the British to do as a vital step to establish EU governance of the regions. He said,

> 'My task here today is to give you a brief overview from a European perspective on the issue of regional devolution and regional autonomy. My task in the Commission consists of participating in the drafting of what is called a White Paper on European Governance which President Prodi has announced as one of his four priorities of his Commission.'

De Rynck stated that the EU Commission has 'sole responsibility in environment, Regional, Transport and Energy Policy, to develop and propose legislation to the national Ministers and to the European parliament.'

Showing his ignorance of the treaty of Rome, Commission Decisions and EU Regulations he remarked

> 'I don't think there is any master plan in Brussels – at least I have never seen the master plan – to regionalise or to carve up the member states . . .'[4]

That was the one and only public occasion to which the EU Commission sent a representative. The Commission, realising that there is substantial British opposition, has stepped out of the limelight, and wisely if it wishes to succeed.

The Bishops explain

Canon Richard Wheeler, the Diocesan Officer for Social Responsibility, explained how the Bishop of St Albans, the Rt. Rev. Christopher Herbert, came to chair the East of England Constitutional Convention. He wrote,

> 'We were approached by high-ranking officials of the East of England Regional Assembly and the government to help them develop a democratic debate about the need for regional government in the East of England. We agreed because we wished to align our activity with them as part of our policy of tracking social developments against a background of our involvement in the local community in the context of our own faith commitment'.[5]

No doubt the Bishop of St Albans was perfectly sincere in his view. It may have been embarrassing for the Bishop when the democratic 'debate' proved to be one-sided.

Were the 'officials' from the Regional Assembly civil servants as the Canon's wording implies? If so, why were civil servants heavily involved in issues of democracy, which should be the domain of politicians and voters?

The Bishop of Durham initiated a debate advocating devolution to the English regions in the House of Lords. He raised the issue of local alienation because of centralised power in Westminster.

> 'I long to see the people of the North East, which is the region that I know best, take a full part in the decisions that will shape their destiny. For generations they have been oppressed and have often lived desperate lives, dependent on others who seem have all the power.'[6]

The Bishop launched the campaign in the North East for an

elected Regional Assembly in St Nicholas Church, Durham on 14th September 2002. Answering letters critical of his activity he wrote,

> 'I see no danger to the identity of England in all this. Indeed, I believe that strong regions will provide a strong nation, well able to hold its own in any future developments of the European Union.'

In April 2004 to prepare for the referendum in the North East when bishops overtly campaigning for votes would be unseemly, the Bishop of Durham handed over the chairmanship to John Tomaney, Professor of Regional Governance at the Centre for Urban and Regional Development Studies at Newcastle University. Professor Tomaney is one of many academics at British universities studying regionalism and the EU.[7]

In his farewell statement the Bishop of Durham said,

> 'I have been a fervent believer in the case for a regional government for the North East of England since I became involved with the campaign six years ago . . . The governance of this region needs to be modernised to adapt to the ever-changing demands of the global market and to provide high quality political leadership for economic regeneration. The campaign will bring forward smart and energetic people to show that this region can forge its own destiny in the modern world.'[8]

The Bishop of Exeter, the Very Rev Michael Langrish, explained his role,

> 'In my comments on the Today programme on Ascension Day, I drew attention to the fact that regional governance is already in existence. It takes

the form of a large number of non-elected quangos, not directly accountable to the people whom they are there to serve, employing a large number of civil servants, and with responsibility for a very large budget. It is my firm belief that if such a tier of government is to exist, it should exist in a form which involves democratic accountability and a far greater level of public participation.

'I made the point that devolution means the transfer of power and money, from Westminster to the lowest possible level of government. I expressed the view that should any new Regional Assembly take one single power from county councils, or lead to additional local taxation, this would be seen as evidence not of devolution, but of further centralisation which has so far eroded the standing of local government for many years.'

In October 2002, members of his congregation asked the Bishop of Exeter why he continued to chair the South West Constitutional Convention when so many people opposed assemblies. He retorted, 'They are Nazis'. Taken aback, they asked if he thought all who opposed regional assemblies were Nazis. He answered 'Yes'. Subsequently the Bishop of Exeter resigned as chairman of the South West Constitutional Convention because of ill health but is now its President.[9]

Praying to the Wrong God?
The Bishops appear to have been drawn into a highly contentious political debate because they have taken up what they see as the issue of local alienation in a highly centralised body politic.

Yet there may another less worthy aspect to this. Is the

Church of England receiving a reward in return for such a high profile and risky political role? There is no certain answer. The Church may believe that the EU could one day introduce a EU-wide Church Tax. In some EU countries, for example Germany and Sweden, a percentage of national taxation goes to the churches. At a stroke this would solve the Church of England's financial crisis.

Unfortunately for the Church of England, the EU Commission's *Soul for Europe* programme leaves little doubt that the Church is being used to lull the population and that the Church will have no role in the future EU.[10] The proposed EU Constitution even failed to acknowledge Europe's Christian heritage: the Preamble referred only to

> 'drawing inspiration from the cultural, humanist and religious inheritance of Europe'.[11]

Perhaps the Church of England should remember that old refrain, if you sup with the devil . . .

Charities going beyond the charitable

The two charities helping to fund the Constitutional Conventions and thus a Yes to regional government are the Andrew Wainwright Reform Trust and the Joseph Rowntree Reform Trust. They are therefore helping to fund the Labour government's political agenda.

The Andrew Wainwright Reform Trust sponsors the Southwest Constitutional Convention, which is largely run by Liberal Democrats who support the aims of the EU. This trust also backs campaigns such as Charter 88, which seeks to dismantle the British constitution, again in favour of the EU. Charter 88's main financier is the Joseph Rowntree Reform Trust.

The government and local authorities are intertwined with two other charities pursuing a government agenda. *Forum for the Future*, founded by the Greens in 1996 with Jonathon Porritt as its Programme Director, is partly government funded. *Forum* campaigns for 'sustainable development', a EU battle cry, and says that

> 'in partnership with local authorities, local strategic partnerships and regional and sub-regional organisations, we support elected members, policy makers and practitioners in their work to join up policy and delivery.'

In 2002 *Forum* launched *Regional Futures*, also a charity and described as the learning network for the English regions.[12] Its members are the Regional Assemblies, Regional Development Agencies and the Government Offices. It is funded jointly by the Esmée Fairbairn Foundation, and by the taxpayer in the guise of the Department for Environment Food and Rural Affairs' Environmental Action Fund and regional organisations.

Even Peter Mandelson, the former Trade and Industry Secretary, was given a £35,000 ($65,000) grant by the Joseph Rowntree Reform Trust, to campaign for political devolution. After Mandelson was forced to resign from the Cabinet for a second time because of questionable dealings, he reinvented himself as a champion of the North East, the region of his constituency. He said he believed that in the wake of devolution for Scotland and Wales, parts of England felt 'ignored'; and unless there were devolution within England the constitution would be left 'dangerously unbalanced'. Shortly afterwards he became a EU Commissioner.

This charitable role is surely highly questionable.

CHAPTER 7

How Taxpayers Pay to Persuade Themselves

The heart of it all

At the heart of regional government is the Deputy Prime Minister's Regional Co-ordination Unit, created in April 2001. It is the Whitehall command centre for the Government Office network.

Funding for one year alone, 2004-5, was £10.5 million ($18.8 m).[1] The Government Offices in the regions, with staff from ten Central Government departments, had running costs in 2004–05 of £4.5 million ($8 m).

The Campaign for the English Regions and the Constitution Unit

The British government has created organisations just to promote regionalisation and at the taxpayers' expense. These quangos, operating at arms length from the government, are bureaucracies with no democratic check and no accountability to the people who ultimately pay the bills.

A pivotal government organisation is the Campaign for the English Regions (CFER). Despite its role, it is scarcely known.[2] The CFER campaigns jointly with the Local Government Information Unit, also taxpayer funded, to promote power for the regions. It published *Regions That Work* in May 2004, a report that argued the EU's line of tackling regional inequalities.

The only published accounts, for the year ending August 31st 2002, show that over two thirds of the CFER budget of nearly £150,000 ($280,000) was contributed by the two charities backing the Constitutional Conventions, the Joseph Rowntree Reform Trust[3] and the Andrew Wainwright Reform Trust plus the trade union, UNISON. UNISON also provides a free office in its building in Newcastle upon Tyne. It was UNISON that made such a substantial contribution to the Yes vote in Wales.

The CFER used to be of no fixed abode, moving from region to region, but in 2005 it settled in the West Midlands, perhaps because that is the home of its chairman, George Morran. Morran appears to be financially dependent on government funding. He has two other jobs: Project Director of the West Midlands Constitutional Convention, government funded, and at the Constitution Unit, University College, London University, indirectly government funded.

The Constitution Unit is yet another example of an organisation, which pretends to be above politics. Its literature describes it as the UK's foremost *independent* think tank on constitutional change and is non-partisan. That is false. It is mainly funded by the Economic and Social Research Council (ESRC) Devolution and Constitutional Change programme based at the University of Birmingham, itself government funded by the British taxpayer with £4.7 million ($8.7 m).[4]

The Constitution Unit is running a five-year research programme of 12 projects. All those projects fall within the government's agenda for devolution and regionalisation.

The programme is totally one sided. No government-funded project at any British university is investigating a contrary view.

The Future of
EU Regional
Policy
Post 2006

L'avenir de la
Politique régionale
de l'UE après 2006

Views of the English
Regions Network

Points de Vue du réseau
des régions Anglaises

ERN
English Regions
Network

English Regions Network pamphlet in English and French

The Local Government Information Unit

The Local Government Information Unit (LGIU) works hand in glove with the Campaign for the English Regions to promote regional power over important policy areas, which are within the competence of the European Union, not of national governments. These are

- o Planning and spatial strategies
- o Allocating housing capital investment
- o Transport
- o Economic development, job creation and business support
- o Determining a regional skills strategy, including funding adult learning
- o Rural issues including land management and forestry

The LGIU describes itself as an independent think tank but it is no such thing. The LGIU is funded by its members, who are local authorities using taxpayers' money, and five of the UK's largest trade unions.

The English Regions Network: an expensive liaison

The English Regions Network (ERN) calls itself 'the collective voice of the regions'.[5] This quango is so 'collective' that voting is unnecessary. According to its constitution it operates by consensus and policy *emerges*. Each region takes it in turn to manage the ERN's affairs, so it has no headquarters.

The Labour government set up the ERN in 2001 as an umbrella organisation for all the regional assemblies. It is intended to bring members and officials together 'into an integrated framework' and liase between the regional assemblies and the government.[6]

The ERN is funded from the Office of the Deputy Prime Minister (ODPM): it received £1 million in its first year (2001–2002) and £200,000 for each subsequent year.

Additionally, the ODPM gave the eight regional assemblies £5 million a year for the first two years (2001 to 2003) and in 2004 to 2005 nearly £18 million.[7]

In addition to liaison, the ERN carries out projects under four headings: engaging social and economic partners; addressing the economic agenda and scrutinising regional development agencies; the assemblies' sustainable development role; and inter-regional collaboration. It has already lobbied its own paymaster, the government, on air transport, planning reform and the White Paper, *Your Region, Your Choice*. And it lobbies the EU Commission for more grants.

Through the ERN, regional assembly members regularly meet the EU's Regional Policy Commissioner, either in Brussels or on his rare visits to the English regions.

Despite the word English in its name and its apparently domestic interests, the ERN produces brochures in both English and French to promote 'cross-border, trans-national and inter-regional initiatives'.[8] This is another questionable use of British taxpayers' money.

The ERN funds the regional arm of charities such as Age Concern's Regions for All Ages. Age Concern and other major charities also in receipt of government money must therefore carry out part of the government's agenda. That turns these charities into quangos.

The full extent of what the ERN does and for whose benefit with its millions of pounds from the British taxpayer is unclear.

Gateways to the assemblies, Civic Forums

The Scottish Constitutional Convention did not disband after its single aim of a Scottish parliament was achieved. It turned into the unwieldy Scottish Civic Forum with over 250 members. According to its website it is a 'facilitator of stakeholder input into the Parliament and the Executive but particularly the executive' and a 'gateway between Scottish Government, civic organisations and wider society.'⁹ The Scottish Executive funds this non-statutory body: that is the taxpayer again.

There is a London Civic Forum too, which is funded by the London mayor's office with an annual budget of £200,000 ($360,000), more taxpayers' money. Its Council of 50 and executive committee of 10 'advise' the mayor.

Membership of the Civic Forums is only for what are called societal groups. That is business organisations, community councils, religious groups, trade unions, the voluntary sector and professional organisations.

In Scotland the Forum is not open to local authorities, political parties, government agencies or for-profit companies.

In 2003 the Forum set up a network of regional co-ordinators in the Highlands and Islands, Mid Scotland and Fife, Glasgow, the Lothians, West Scotland and Central Scotland. Co-ordinators organise events on government consultations in their area, and offer the chance for input into national government decisions at a local level.

The Welsh equivalents are called Partnership Councils. According to the Welsh First Minister, Alun Michael, they embody *three golden threads*: local government (largely the Welsh Local Government Association, National Park, police and fire authorities), business (mainly the Welsh Assembly, TUC, and Business Wales), and the voluntary sector (the Welsh Assembly, the Wales Council for Voluntary Action and 21 others).

So a total of 79 people from these various organisations act as a 'gateway' to the National Assembly for Wales.

Presumably if the Constitutional Conventions in the English regions succeed in their appointed tasks of creating elected assemblies, they too will turn into Civic Forums, expensive gateways to the assemblies.

Taxpayers may like to ask why these gateways are necessary.

Any popular support?

Nowhere in England has there been more than marginal support or interest in regional assemblies, as the 2004 referendum in the North East of England resoundingly demonstrated. What support there has been comes mainly from those benefiting or hoping to benefit financially from taxpayer funded jobs.

Because of minimal interest, the government's 'soundings exercise' to explain regional assemblies to the people, which began in December 2002, had to be extended twice. In the North East, which the government thought was likely to be the most enthusiastic about regions, only 38 people replied to the consultation exercise: 30 of those favoured an elected assembly, eight were against.

In the Eastern region, over an eighteen-month period, 79 individuals and organisations replied with one individual and one parish council supporting an elected regional assembly and 43 against. The other inquirers either did not express a definite opinion or merely sought information.[10]

Even the meaning of the word 'debate' has suffered a reinterpretation. Voters had to be convinced of the government's case *before* they were allowed to hear the arguments in favour of regional assemblies. Outrageously, at some meetings individuals thought to be opposed to regional assemblies were refused entry unless they first signed a document agreeing to their existence.[11] Bill and Ann Woodhouse of Dorset were two of many who refused to sign but successfully argued at the door for the democratic right to entry to hear the case for regional assemblies.

In an exchange in the House of Commons during the Third Reading of the Regions Bill in 2003 Desmond Swayne, the Conservative MP for the New Forest, stated that

'. . . the South East region has 8 million electors.

Eighteen responses were received in favour of a Regional Assembly. In Hampshire, there are more than 960,000 electors – not people, electors – but there were only two respondents in favour of the proposals. The Ministers know their uphill task. They therefore have a mechanism: any response whatever is counted as interest in favour of a referendum. The fact that someone might be wholly against an Assembly, and might write to say so, will nevertheless be counted as someone expressing an interest in a referendum. Our task in securing a petition will not be nearly so easy as the method that the Ministers have devised for themselves.

Mr. Andrew Turner (Isle of Wight): I am shocked and amazed at the implicit duplicity of Ministers if, as my hon. Friend asserts, they should count a clear expression of objection to a regional Assembly as an argument in favour of a referendum. I know of the huge amount of work that has been done by our colleagues, MEPs representing the South East, in campaigning against a referendum. Is he saying that Ministers are genuinely taking such expressions against as expressions of interest in a referendum being held?

Mr. Swayne: . . . The position is precisely as he fears.'[12]

Yet the Deputy Prime Minister, John Prescott, announced that a consultation exercise in the South West had shown overwhelming public interest in the idea. Speaking in the House of Commons, he said

'I think that the regional assemblies have been

quite successful. *[Laughter.]* I take as one indication of that the active participation of Tory councillors on the assemblies. In fact, more than 160 Tory councillors sit on the boards. They think that they are doing a good job, and we will retain them. No doubt the referendum will provide people with a good opportunity to state whether they want to go further and have a regional referendum. The indications are that well over 60 per cent of people in the south-west want to have a referendum.'[13]

CHAPTER 8

Regions have Limited Powers

Creating the brand

English regions have no history, no tradition, no homogeneity and therefore no 'brand'. Or in the language of the EU, they have no demos.

So one of the first things the new English regional assemblies did was to hire advertising agents to create a brand. Taxpayers' money is spent on building the brand, just like soap powder, and then the assemblies can 'advocate' them.

Regions have targeted well-known 'local' individuals to be ambassadors for the new brand 'on the world stage' and without any reference to the UK. Regions are treated almost like countries in their own right.

Here is an extract from one such letter:

> 'By 2010 the East of England Region aims to be one of the top regions in Europe. Made up of Bedfordshire, Cambridgeshire, Essex, Hertfordshire, Norfolk and Suffolk, the East of England is a diverse and fascinating region and one that you are closely associated with.
>
> 'Key to its future success will be our ability to

promote the East of England on the world stage. One way that our goal will be achieved, for the good of all who live, work, visit and invest in the region is by building a strong brand for the region. This brand is called 'East of England – space for ideas').

'In 2004 we, the East of England Development Agency (EEDA) have some very exciting plans for the brand. And this is where we would like your help. A diverse mix of companies, individuals and organisations has already committed their assistance, and as a recognised member of the regional community I would like to invite you to become an East of England ambassador.

'I will call your offices over the next week to explore the possibility of setting up a 15-minute East of England – space for ideas introduction meeting to talk you through both the commercial and non-commercial opportunities available. Please be assured that any commitment you do make will take up a minimum amount of your time. If, in the meantime, you have any questions please do not hesitate to contact me . . .

'Through collective effort and commitment we hope:

'to make the East of England a world-class economy, renowned for its knowledge base, the creativity and enterprise of its people and the quality of life of all who live and work here' *East of England strategic review goal 2002*

'Ambitious as it might be, we are all 100% committed to our goal and would ask you to recognise both the personal and community based rewards of investing in the East of England's future.'[1]

The master plan?

The East of England Region was right: the EU vision is of 'an integrated Europe of the Regions and the Cities'.[2] That vision notably fails to mention countries.

All regions both in the UK and across Europe will eventually report to Brussels alone and not to countries. Countries will be reduced to lines on a map, without substance, and of historical interest only. Writing in *The Times*, Roger Boyes commented of Germany that

> 'Regional *Länder* governments now have more contact with Brussels than with Berlin.'[3]

An inner group in each assembly carries out a limited agenda within parameters set by the EU Commission, though it is unlikely that they are aware of the source of what they do. Most assembly members are merely a talking shop and will remain so, elected or not. The considerable costs of this are laid out in the next chapter.

Once 'legitimised' by elections, the English regions may eventually acquire similar powers to the German Länder. Each of the 16 Land has a judiciary, a legislature, and some tax raising powers. They are sovereign within their own territory with their own identity, policies and laws.

For example, German Basic Law forbids one Land from merging with another (article 79 (3)). No amendments to the Basic Law may detract from the Länder's quality of statehood and article 28 specifically guarantees them 'the right of self-government'. Each Land has the power to administer and execute laws (article 30).

Critically the Länder only have the right to make laws on

matters not conferred on the Federation (article 70). Their freedom is therefore severely circumscribed.

Scotland already has similar powers to the Länder and Wales aspires to them. The Queen's Speech in May 2005 included a Government of Wales Bill to increase the legislative powers of the National Assembly of Wales.

Limited power of the English regions today

English regional assemblies today have only three functions: planning, lobbying Brussels for money and as we have already seen creating their own identity.

The South East England Regional Assembly (SEERA) claims three functions: accountability, advocacy and regional planning. All three claims are bizarre.

- The Assembly is not elected so it can only be accountable to its paymasters, the British government and the European Union.
- SEERA's claim to advocacy, usually a term used of lawyers, can only be to promote itself and its masters' agendas.
- The EU controls the parameters of regional planning, so SEERA is an agent of Brussels' planning.

Not our land but EU land

All regions are preparing the first EU statutory plans for the 10 years 2006 to 2016 with reviews extending to 2026. They are also contributing to the EU Environmental Action Plan and the EU's transport policy. These plans form part of the EU's Spatial Strategies including plans for their sub regions. They include a range of services at present provided by Government Offices, county councils and district councils.

Controlling how the land is used, the planning process, effectively means controlling the country. Setting the principles for land use has already passed to Brussels. The *European Spatial Development Perspective* (ESDP) is premised on 'a balanced and sustainable spatial structure' for an integrated European Union.[4]

The EU is attempting the grand vision. Its plans try to integrate every aspect of land use, including transport, all environmental and many social issues. Much is already proscribed in EU directives, now written into national law.

One important result is the diminution of democracy and the ability of local people to control local planning matters.

The way this works in London is that the boroughs, elected authorities, approve planning applications. But those plans may be subject to a series of negatives from higher authorities. They cannot say yes, they can only say no. London boroughs have to refer all planning applications 'that are considered of potential strategic importance' to the Mayor of London. The Mayor cannot approve them but at meetings normally held every two weeks he personally refuses those that do not fit the London Plan.

In turn, the civil servants of the Government Office for London are responsible, on behalf of the Secretary of State, for ensuring that the London Mayoral strategies are consistent with national policies. Again this power is limited either to refusal or to direct changes.

The Government Office for London also represents London's interest in European Spatial Planning, and in the development of EU planning and policy.

Thus it is fair to say that the London Plan, the Mayor's Spatial Development Strategy, for policies for building and land use, is part of the European Spatial Development Perspectives.

It is also telling that the London Plan is organised by EU sub regions, not by boroughs.

Is the Mayor of London working for Londoners or for Brussels?

Outside London, elected county councils are already 'assisting' the unelected regional assemblies to prepare the inaugural Regional Spatial Strategy (RSS) and sub-regional strategies. Macro decisions on housing and transport are now out of local and democratic control. Plans have to fit the regional strategic plan, and that in turn fits the EU plan.

Thus, strategic planning has been transferred from elected county and city councils to the unelected regional assemblies.

The government was fully aware of likely public disquiet: to avoid widespread and strident objections, the 2001 Green Paper did not go to a White Paper as is the norm, but was introduced directly in the 2003 Queen's Speech, and quickly enacted as the Planning and Compulsory Purchase Act.[5]

Such is the British government's disdain for debate. But it goes further.

The government damned established county and local council planning as 'not sufficiently inclusive and (it) does not propose to recognise them for purposes of the new regional spatial strategies.'[6] This is even more curious as these councils are properly elected.

The House of Commons Select Committee debating the Green Paper reasonably recommended that decisions on regional planning should be taken by groups of democratically elected members of local authorities. Wider interests should be consulted but they should not make decisions. Only when *elected* regional assemblies are set up, should they take over regional planning functions.

The Labour government agreed with MPs that regions with *elected* assemblies should take over responsibility for regional planning. But disagreed with MPs that everywhere else decisions on planning should be taken only by elected local authorities:

'In five of the eight [English] regions draft regional
planning guidance is the responsibility of the more
inclusive regional chambers.'

That word *inclusive* does not refer to democracy, to one-
man one vote, as it should. It refers to lobby groups and
vested interests, the 'stakeholders', giving an inside track to
some companies, charities and quangos which include representatives of vested interests like the CBI and trade unions.

Through the planning system the EU can introduce other
policies. It is indeed a most insidious form of takeover. The
most visible has been the enforced the use of the metric system,
which has almost totally overwhelmed the imperial system. All
planning has to be in hectares, kilometres, metres and so
forth.[7] Acres, miles and yards are out.

The Rape of Norfolk and Oxfordshire

Here are examples of properly elected county councils and
district councils being over-ridden.

The East of England Regional Assembly approved a plan in
February 2004 to build nearly half a million new houses in the
Eastern Region over the next 20 years. In Norfolk alone,
72,400 new homes will be built.

The elected Norfolk County Council no longer has any
influence over this. But it did demand that the government
should fund roads and services for the new communities,
particularly creating a dual carriageway on the congested A11
and improving the A47.

The unelected East of England Regional Assembly turned
down Norfolk County Council. To qualify as a dual carriageway the A11 would have to be defined as a trans-European
link between major centres of population. But until the new
houses are built, the A11 must stay as a single carriageway.

The South East England Regional Assembly agreed in July

2004 to build between 34,000 and 36,000 new homes every year in the region. In Oxfordshire alone this would add another 40,000 new homes over the next 20 years on top of existing local plans, whether people in Oxfordshire want them or not.

The proposed numbers are so big that people in Oxfordshire fear the Green Belt will be invaded (land around towns and villages protected from development), existing towns will explode, arguably the very essence of the county will be destroyed and it will no longer be a pleasant place to live.

In this case, the South East England Regional Assembly voted two to one against the plan and now has to select a new target figure. The Assembly cannot reject the plan completely.

Local fears are proving only too right. The regional assemblies are cancelling Green Belt designation: 2,500 acres are built over every year. John Prescott has already rubber-stamped 162 planning applications in Green Belts, and changes in national planning rules have downgraded the status of the Green Belt.

'Regenerating' the sub-regions

The EU has found a way to extend its influence over planning right down to bus timetables. It now gives grants to 'regenerate sub-regions.' That word regeneration normally has the specific meaning of giving a new lease of life to decaying infrastructure, but in the EU context, it appears to be used broadly. 'Regeneration' enables the EU to claim that it is carrying out the regional policy of the treaty of Rome by eliminating regional disparities.

Yet it also allows the EU to involve itself in nearly every nook and cranny of local life.

The EU's Market Towns Initiative is a twin to the regional plans, and like them takes both ten year and 20-year views.[8] The Initiative enables the EU for the first time to influence overall local planning, as opposed to simply giving grants for individual projects.

Under this scheme, EU grants have already been given to over 220 towns throughout England for individual projects 'to provide a *gateway* to funding programmes that will really make things happen' or ' to create vibrant, healthy and sustainable Market and Coastal Towns'.[9] That word *gateway* proliferates in all EU planning: the town of Saltash is now 'the gateway to Cornwall.'

From a EU planning point of view, the significance of these chosen towns is that they provide access to goods and services for the surrounding area, which neatly extends the scope of the project. Eurostat, the EU's statistical office, defines market towns very broadly as those with a population of between 2,000 and 20,000.

Outlined in the Rural White Paper of 2000, the Market Towns Initiative embraces every aspect of town and country life.[10] It includes the standard EU method of creating lots of partnerships, and ensuring the local plan fits into the regional plan, which in turn fits the EU's plan. Planning goes from the major, like housing estates, to the minor such as signs at the local railway station. Grants are available for all.

Elected local government has been bypassed.

The British government funded the first three years to the tune of £37 million ($66m) largely through the regional development agencies, and £5 million ($9m) through its quango, the Countryside Agency.[11]

The Countryside Agency assesses the economic, social and environmental strengths and weaknesses of a town and its surrounding area using its so-called Healthcheck Handbooks and Healthbook Action Plans.[12] Healthchecks were described in the Rural White Paper as measuring 'a variety of physical improvements as well as in renewed local pride, with the community taking and keeping control of its town's destiny.'

The extent of government and quango involvement in the Market Towns Initiative is broad and costly. For example in the East of England it includes:

- ○ Action for Market Towns
- ○ East of England Development Agency
- ○ English Heritage
- ○ Government Office of the Eastern Region (Go-East)
- ○ Department of the Environment, Food and Rural Affairs (Defra)
- ○ Sport England
- ○ The Legal Services Commission
- ○ Rural Action East representing the Rural Community Councils
- ○ East of England Tourist Board (EETB)

The Market Towns Initiative has given rise to among other things: exchanges between project officers from different towns, Learning Networks, newsletters, seminars, Skills workshops and the designation of Beacon Towns and Beacon Projects.

According to the Rural White Paper,

> 'the Countryside Agency will identify a national beacon towns network . . . featuring 10–20 towns to demonstrate the range of different problems and challenges which market towns experience and from other towns can learn.'

Under the banner of Beacon Projects, virtually anything can be called Beacon, right down to the local golf or tennis club. And with the imprimatur of *Beacon* come EU grants.

'Devolving' national government: a work in progress

The British government is in the process of regionalising the administration of many other government functions, while still remaining responsible for them. Some functions are moved down from Central Government. Others are moved up from county councils. Other national functions have already gone to Brussels or will do so shortly.[13]

Government Offices in the regions already carry out work for ten Whitehall departments and it would be but a short hop to transfer those responsibilities to the regional assemblies.[14]

Here are examples of responsibilities removed from counties to the regions:

○ Museums, libraries and archives, now called the Museum, Library and Archive Council (MLA), have 'developed a shared strategic framework with our key strategic partners the English Regional Agencies'. County archives are now regional. All public libraries provide large racks prominently displayed for Brussels' propaganda or Public Information Points and entirely one sided.

○ Tourism is already the responsibility of regional development agencies

○ The Fire and Rescue Service, until now organised by counties, is about to be reorganised into the much bigger regional units at vast expense with new regional headquarters' buildings plus the cost of dislocation.[15] 46 command and control centres, close to the people they serve, are to be replaced by nine centres with fewer staff on duty to answer emergency telephone calls. Every region is to have a new building built by the private sector and rented to the Fire Service. New equipment will add to the cost. Many in the fire services have called for an independent review because of the way the Deputy Prime Minister's Office is introducing this revolution, the lack of consultation about the heavy costs, where the new headquarters will be sited and the dangers of increasing the distance from those needing the service.

○ When it is politic to do so the police are almost certain to be regionalised. That has been discussed informally for some years within police forces. The ramifications are considerable: the most obvious is the elimination of the 43 constabularies of England and Wales with their local accountabilities. Regional police may eventually work to the command of Europol, the EU police agency.

In due course, regional assemblies may have even more powers dealing directly with Brussels, most alarmingly on policing and justice. The EU has already orchestrated its lobbyists to chorus for regions to have direct access to the European Court of Justice, bypassing national judiciaries (see page 137).

The government White Paper, *Justice for All,* set out regional administration for the law courts in England and Wales with all courts reporting to a single agency for the first time.[16] From April 2005, all law courts were amalgamated into a single executive agency, Her Majesty's Courts Service, with 20,000 staff and a budget of about £1 billion ($2.8 bn). The government said it would save money and provide better management. Centralising and making bigger has had the opposite effect: the new Courts Service has spawned hundreds of committees and sub-committees, which arguably do nothing at all to improve justice in the UK.

In November 2003, the Department of Constitutional Affairs in the face of strong opposition had to announce a temporary climb down in its plans to regionalise the Crown and County Courts, but only until 2006.

At first the old system of Crown and County Courts in six circuits will continue under the new Agency, but with regional management added to match the nine 'English' regions plus

Wales. Scotland has its independent judiciary; it was never absorbed into the UK.

As the government put it,

> 'regional offices will increasingly be joined up with other government services at a regional level. We do not want the courts to be left behind in that, and many of our justice partners – the Children and Family Court Advisory and Support Service, the National Probation Service, the Prison Service and, informally, the Crown Prosecution Service – are already aligning with the government office regions.'[17]

Imposing regions on the courts created two boundary problems: Cheshire was to move from the North Wales circuit to the North West Region, and Hampshire and the Isle of Wight from the South West to the South East. Facing strong resistance from the judiciary, the government backed down.[18]

But the government had *already* decided that on review in 2006–07 the old boundaries will be scrapped for

> 'compelling reasons . . . the regional agenda is developing . . . the greater need for a well-organised, cross-cutting and integrated criminal justice system able to work readily with other public services remains an important part of our reform agenda, hence the decision that has been made.'[19]

Some review!

Without doubt the magistrates courts will in due course follow the police into regions. At present these courts are run by 42 independent magistrates courts committees, conveniently with the same boundaries as the police authorities and the Crown Prosecution Service.

The regions of Scotland and Wales

Some Scots and Welsh may hope and believe that with their own parliament and assembly they are well on the way to independent nationhood. They are not. Scotland and Wales are merely regions within the EU and are described in Brussels' literature as *Scotland in Europe* and *Wales in Europe*. Indeed the Scottish administration itself refers to *Scotland, European Region of the Future*.[20]

The Scottish Parliament, or to be more accurate the Scottish Regional Assembly, has limited powers. London gives Scotland a £14 billion ($25 bn) block grant.[21] The Scottish Parliament can only vary income tax by 3p up or down (roughly £450 million) and change the format of local council tax, though not the overall level.

Areas reserved to the UK Parliament for decision only include the constitution, foreign policy, defence and security, economic and monetary systems, common trade, employment and social security, and transport safety. The Scots have responsibility for their own health, schools, local government, housing, economic development, transport, law, environment, agriculture, sports and arts.

The Scottish Executive, headed by a First Minister, is drawn from MSPs (Members of the Scottish Parliament) elected by two systems: 73 by first-past-the-post in constituencies and 56 additional members from party lists plus 8 MSPs from each of the eight EU constituencies, all with the standard EU fixed four year terms.

The Welsh revolution was even more limited. Wales has a directly elected Assembly with a £7 billion ($12 bn) budget from London, but no power to tax. The Assembly sets limited policies, passes secondary legislation and redesigns quangos in Wales. Its 60 members are elected every four years: 40 from constituencies and five from each of the four EU constituencies.

In 2004, the Richard Commission on the Powers and Electoral Arrangements of the National Assembly for Wales reported at length. Not surprisingly, it advocated more not less power for Wales.[22] It proposed limited extra powers including 20 more Assembly members and some primary legislative power along the Scottish model.

Just as the MP Tam Dalyell had predicted in 1976, both the Scottish Parliament and the National Assembly for Wales are calling for yet more power.

Can the United Kingdom survive that and still remain united?

CHAPTER 9

Taxpayers Foot a Heavy Bill

How wrong can John Prescott be?

The cost of 'a pint of beer and a bag of fish and chips' per person would cover the running costs of a Regional Assembly. So claimed John Prescott. [1] On this, as on everything else to do with regions, the deputy prime minister was seriously mistaken.

As predicted in the 1973 Kilbrandon Report, the new tier of government is very expensive. A conservative estimate of the costs just to reorganise the UK into regions is over £4 billion ($7 bn) and the annual running costs have *already* doubled with worse to come. New buildings in London, Edinburgh and Cardiff cost well over £600 million ($1.08 bn). No doubt there will be many more new buildings.

Here are the latest available figures.

❍ In Wales, the running costs of the National Assembly were £177 million with 3,777 staff in 2002–3. The cost, compared with running the old Welsh Office, has gone up two and half times in five years and staffing levels by 63 per cent. On a like for like basis the cost doubled. The Assembly building cost £55 million. To preserve the excellent view for civil servants working in the office tax-

City Hall, the London Assembly, by Tower Bridge

The Debating Chamber, The Scottish Parliament, Image © Scottish
Parliamentary Corporate Body – 2005

payers paid an extra £750,000 to buy a piece of land next to it.[2]

○ The Welsh First Minister, Rhodri Morgan, decided to open Welsh 'embassies', called Wales International Centres. The first opened in 2003 in the Chrysler Building, New York. More may follow in San Francisco, Tokyo, Sydney, Singapore and Brussels. According to Mr. Morgan, they will provide a 'virtual Wales, a focal point for international trade in investment and tourism'. The National Assembly for Wales does not have a remit for international affairs. How can two and a half million Welsh afford this?

○ Members of the National Assembly who live more than 20 miles away are eligible for a free loan to buy accommodation nearby. Even worse, if they make a profit on their new homes they can keep it. Prices have already risen sharply with the influx of assembly members, staff and civil servants.

○ In Scotland, the new Parliament building was originally estimated to cost £40 million but the contract was not even placed with the lowest bidder. Then costs rose to over £430 million. The running costs for the year ending March 2003 were £255 million.

○ The Northern Irish Assembly, even in 'cold storage', costs £800,000 to run every year; each Assembly member is paid a reduced salary of £21,000 plus office costs of £48,000 simply for waiting to govern.

○ The London Assembly's prominent glass and steel building on the Thames, opened by the Queen with the mayors of London, Paris and Berlin and the First Deputy Mayor of Moscow in attendance, cost £120 million. The building has cramped offices and is prone to leaks. Designed for 400 staff, it already houses more than 630. The hunt is on for a second building. The running costs are over £60 million a year, with many publicity officers to sell non-policies to the taxpayer. A further £300 million is channelled through the London Development Agency.

o Londoners' council tax has doubled in just four years to pay for it. Costs are still rising sharply.

o Each of the eight English regional assemblies already costs *well over* the original estimate £25 million a year to run, a grand total of £200 million a year.

o Part time chairmen of those assemblies earn about £40,000 a year for two days a week.

o All unelected assembly members are paid expenses, which can easily top £500 a week plus travel costs, and they spread the light work load of the day across the free lunch thus doubling their expenses. There is plenty of committee work to augment the expenses some of it requiring travel to London.

o Each assembly member, if and when elected, will be paid £35,000 a year plus expenses for a very part-time job.

o While the government estimated in *Your Region, Your Choice* that about 200 staff would be needed for each assembly, some of whom would be transferred from the Government Offices, those numbers have already been exceeded. In the South East, GOSE has two buildings in Guildford and Chatham, employs over 500 staff and is recruiting heavily.

o The South West Regional Assembly alone employs 54 full-time staff in Taunton with a wage bill of more than £2 million. Multiplying that by the eight assemblies gives staffing of well over 400 and a wage bill of £16 million. The Regional Developments Agencies (RDAs) employ 200 to 300 staff each, making at least 2,000 in the nine Agencies.

o A further 20,000 staff from London and the South East

will transfer to the new regions over three to five years (starting in 2005) particularly from the Treasury, the Department for Work and Pensions and the Ministry of Defence. More buildings will be needed.

Ironically county councils are paying towards their own demise. Regional assemblies are partly funded by all local authorities and partly by government. For example, the South West Regional Assembly levies 'subscriptions' from the counties and districts in the Southwest of more than £1 million of taxpayers' money. Each district council is paying about £5,000 and county councils about £20,000 a year to fund the Regional Assembly whether their voters wish it or not. They have never been asked.

Nor is it just the cost of *construction*: *destruction* is expensive too. During the last local government reorganisation, abolishing a single county council, Humberside, and then restructuring local district councils, cost £53 million ($95m) in one-off costs.[3]

Bribed with our own money

'One of the most visible signs on the ground of the benefits of EU membership is getting some of our own money back for EU projects', the British government bizarrely claimed. The government has admitted that acquiring EU money has been 'the catalyst for strengthened links between the regions and the EU'.[4]

Just after the Second World War, when the EU project was in its infancy, the emphasis was on town twinning, which needed only limited financial resources. To date there about 30,000 twinning links across Europe, all promoted an integrated Europe.[5] From 1960, when the first EEC structural fund was set up, the bait became generous grants.

The grant system is expensive and bureaucratic.

Nonetheless, it has successfully made local authorities reorganise, and most now have European departments to promote the EU so that they can get some of the British taxpayers' money back in the form of grants.

Those grants ensure that local politicians turn to Brussels with their hands outstretched. They claim, quite reasonably, that they are doing so in the financial interests of their voters. Unfortunately there are strings attached to the grants. In the longer term voters may lose all control and ultimately their country.

Every British region with a coastline, which the EU calls Border Regions, gets even more money for 'cross border' projects to help break down the nation state. Only the East and West Midlands lack a coastline and cannot be Border Regions. Border Regions were highlighted in that vital EEC Communication of 1969 to be supervised directly by the Commission (see page 22).

Half the money the British taxpayer hands over to the EU covers its bloated administration. The EU gives the other half to projects of which it approves but only after the project is completed. The working capital has to be provided by the nation state, but of course at a further cost.

British regions flocking to Brussels, not to London

Brussels rivals Vienna in the glorious days of the Austro-Hungarian Empire. Over 170 regions and local authorities from across Europe beg for money and favours.

All regions must have an office in the EU's capital and direct contact with the European Commission. EU law says so. Many counties and local authorities have also opened offices in Brussels over the last 15 years to plead for money at yet more cost to the taxpayer.

None of the British regions has offices in the national capital, London. Brussels is the new capital city and that source of money and favours. Doors can open wide to the European Investment Bank, the European Social Fund, the European Regional Development Fund promoting 'economic and social cohesion', the funds for fishing and farming and the Cohesion Fund for deprived EU countries.

In total, the UK maintains 31 offices in Brussels. The larger ones, called 'sub-national offices', have annual budgets of about £500,000 ($900,000). The smaller ones only have about half a dozen staff. All the Scottish offices are in Scotland House led by Scotland Europa, and all those within the South East England Region in South East England House.

In the future only regions will be allowed to have Brussels' offices. The British counties will have to go home.

The cost to the taxpayer of ten more countries

In May 2004, the centre of gravity for EU grants shifted to Eastern Europe when 10 more countries joined the EU, making 25 countries in all. Yet even before the new countries became members, British taxpayers had already contributed millions for massive infrastructure projects.

In one country alone, Poland, taxpayers paid via the EU's PHARE, SAPARD and ISPA programmes to

o rebuild the Warsaw to Krakow motorway of nearly 250 miles (the A4). Cost: £125 million ($225m).

o update the railway from Siedlce, a city 56 miles east of Warsaw, to Terespol on the Belarus border. Cost: £93 million ($167m).

o build a vast waste and water treatment complex in Szczecin, Poland's seventh largest city of over 400,000 people: water and sewage pipes, pumping and water treatment stations. That is another £125 million ($225m) from taxpayers.

No wonder Poles were keen to join the EU.

The EU now has to spend 50 per cent more on the poorest areas of the new member countries, but do so without reducing aid to the previous poorest regions. Nine out of ten regions in the new EU countries are so poor that they qualify for the highest level of Brussels' aid, Objective One. That is for regions with incomes of less than 75 per cent of the EU average. The Commission estimates it will take so long to close the wealth gap that Poland will continue to receive funding for 30 years and Latvia for nearly 40 years.

Because of the new entrants only Britain's poorest regions, Cornwall and the Highlands and Islands, will still qualify for Brussels' handouts but at a substantially reduced level. In Northern Ireland, the £550 million ($990m) of EU money that helped fund prestige projects will largely dry up. The £275 million ($495m) Peace 2 fund will also end.

In the six years to 2006, Britain will get £9.9 billion ($17.8 bn) of its own money back in 'grants'; but at least £3 billion ($5.4 bn) over the next funding period, 2006 to 2013, will be lost to the new member states.

CHAPTER 10

Democracy Redefined and Downgraded

Trouble ahead: government spurns democracy

'Influence within the EU begins well before the process of formal negotiations between member states and operates through many more channels than the formal EU . . . Assemblies will be able to play their part in the less formal discussions with the institutions of the EU and interests within other member states.'

Your Region, Your Choice §8.18

If the headlines *Government Ditches Democracy* or *Democracy For The Scrap Heap* were blazoned across the front pages of British newspapers or led the television news, the country would suffer alarums and excursions, even riots. Yet democracy in Britain is suffering death by a thousand cuts, the British people have scarcely noticed and the British government is not going to tell them, at least not in a direct manner.

The British government's contempt for the voter could not be clearer. It has espoused 'the post-democratic society' as it is publicly known in Brussels, a phrase which is in everyday speech among EU civil servants and MEPs but only 'over there in Brussels', not 'over here'.

The British government has given strong hints of its conversion to the 'post-democratic society'. It has stated in writing that regional bodies should only 'as far as practicable be democratically accountable'.[1] There is only one conclusion to draw from this: the British government does not believe in democracy and is in the process of abolishing it.

At parish council road shows, government spokesmen readily admit that 'the government wants to move away from a representative democracy to a consultative democracy' (see page 120). The government has already abandoned the ancient British system of open council meetings at which all councillors are equal and information is freely available.

Local authorities (the EU sub regions) now have a cabinet or inner group controlling all council affairs headed by a leader, mayor, or chief executive. Councillors not in that cabinet have little influence and find it difficult to discover what is going on, yet they have been elected by local people to represent them. They are out in the cold and so are their voters.

Power in the parishes (the EU sub sub regions) is about to be similarly centralised and controlled (see page 118).[2]

Oligarchic assemblies with jobs for the boys

This highly centralised system also operates in the regional assemblies: the ordinary assembly member has minimal power and minimal knowledge of what is going on. Should assembly members eventually be elected, that will make no difference at all.

The government may claim that at present two thirds of assembly members are elected councillors, but the voters have not elected them to these assemblies, they have been appointed.

Regional government is oligarchic. Yet the government, and John Prescott in particular, boasted that the regions 'bring decision making closer to those (they) affect'.[3]

A small group will control each regional assembly with a leader and cabinet of up to six members, all with substantial salaries and working full time. Most of them can even be named *before* an election takes place because proportional representation guarantees that the first few on a party list win.

Ordinary elected members, part time, will have minimal power and minimal influence. They will be an expensive chorus.

Greater London Assembly electors count for even less; the electoral structure is a farce. The London mayor has an advisory cabinet, and most of them are appointed.

Inner groups from each region are encouraged to meet and discuss in private with the inner groups of Brussels, most of whom have never faced the electors at the ballot box. They are civil servants owing their loyalty to the EU.

Expensive, powerless assembly members can only be justified as 'jobs for the boys', over 450 of them. No doubt many are keen to keep an easy life style and therefore can be counted on to support the regional government that pays them. If elected, the 'English' regions will have 25 to 35 elected members, but currently while unelected they range from 30 to 60 members; the Greater London Assembly has 25. The Scottish Parliament has 129 MSPs and the Assembly for Wales 60, both representing populations much smaller than London and most other English regions.

The party mafia rules OK

'I used to be a fan of proportional representation, but I am not at all now I have seen it in action. Debate is almost non-existent and no one is apparently accountable to anybody apart from their political party bosses. It is bad news for democracy in this country. Even though we didn't have a free press

under apartheid, the government of that day seemed
to be very much more accountable in parliament.'
Mrs Helen Suzman on South Africa's post-apartheid
constitution[4]

Brussels demands voting by proportional representation
('PR'), not first-past-the post, in European and regional elections across the EU. And there is a good reason for that.

PR is a sinister method of election. PR ensures control by
party: the people are no longer fairly represented. The party
machine selects its favourite sons and daughters and the electors vote for the party list, not the man or woman. Candidates
owe their allegiance not to the voters, but to the party that has
ensured their place on the list and equally can ensure their
political demise and the end of their pay and perks. Where a
party places a candidate on that list ensures his success or
failure.

In the South East region's European elections in 2004, the
ballot papers were over 19 inches long and listed 12 parties. In
small print was a list of the individuals standing for each party
whose names meant little or nothing to the six million voters.
The parties control their lists of candidates and voters can only
choose a party, not a person.

Most winners and losers are a forgone conclusion: the top
few names win, the bottom few lose, with just two or three
candidates in the middle whose fate is uncertain until the
count.

Coalitions are the norm and change is difficult to achieve.
PR ensured that in Scotland the leading party did not have
enough MSPs to form an administration so it did a deal with
the party that came last. Therefore the party the voters *least*
liked became part of the administration. That has been the
experience of all countries operating forms of PR.[5]

Accountability vanishes overnight. Were PR to be used for

UK parliamentary elections then the old cry of 'we can kick them out at the next election' would not work. PR would ensure coalition after coalition and no significant change.

A EU-wide party system is developing. At present it exists only in the European Parliament, plus the two huge advisory groups, the Committee of the Regions and the Economic and Social Committee.

National parties have to join EU parties to get money: Brussels pays for researchers and administration. That bait of money is sufficient to ensure that national parties compromise their principles and are subject to an alien set of rules, just as the British Conservative Party has done by associating itself with the European Peoples Party (EPP) which espouses EU integration. It is yet another way in which the EU seeks to control.

A not so secret ballot: e-government

The EU is promoting electronic voting and electronic consultation backed by choruses from every EU quango and every EU committee.[6]

Concerns have been raised across the Western world about the security of computer voting. Those concerns should be greatest in the EU with its track record of manipulating referendums.

Every part of British central and local government now has committees and teams promoting e-democracy. The Labour government has already opened the door to electoral fraud for the sake of party advantage, bringing the integrity of elections into doubt. Given the outcry about the abuse of postal voting, it is unlikely that there will be much public appetite for e-democracy in the foreseeable future. Nonetheless the government has continued to spend large sums of taxpayers' money on it because the EU agenda demands e-voting some time after 2006.[7]

CHAPTER 11

Cabals Challenge People Power

London: Patronage and corruption the way of the future

Mayor Ken Livingstone of the EU's London Region has the powers of a 21st century baron. His powers are the opposite of John Prescott's claim of power to the people. Livingstone's patronage of jobs carrying large salaries and influence is disturbing. In his personal gift are several million pounds of reward for the 'right' people. His power to appoint is so expansive as to be dictatorial. There are no checks and no balances within the Greater London Assembly on his power other than the threat that he might not be re-elected. There are no term limits. Ken Livingstone can go on and on.

Livingstone personally appoints all 15 members of Transport for London which he chairs; all 15 members plus the chief executive of the London Development Agency; nearly half of the London Fire and Emergency Planning Authority; the whole board of the Cultural Strategy group; the executive and chair of the London Health Commission and many other jobs.

Livingstone can deny freedom of speech. In June 2004, a Cornish trawler tried to sail up the Thames to protest with banners at the Tower of London ahead of the European parliamentary elections. The Port of London Authority at the behest of Livingstone refused the trawler a berth anywhere on the Thames.

Livingstone decides which groups or individuals to support. He chooses to use taxpayers' money for St Patrick's Day celebrations but refuses all others.

What should give even more pause for thought is the mayor's power over the police. The London Mayor appoints just over half of the members of the Metropolitan Police Authority. He has a role in the appointment, discipline and removal of *all* senior police officers.

Is the Mayor above the law?

Yet John Prescott, when Secretary of State for the Environment, Transport and the Regions, told the House of Commons that the Greater London Authority Bill was

> 'about modernising the government of the capital, and about giving power to the people of London, stripping away the shadowy committees, burgeoning bureaucracies and quangos created by our predecessor. The Government were elected on a promise to modernise the way in which Britain is governed. We promised to make our politics more open, more accountable and more inclusive, and relevant to the 21st century. We are delivering on that promise. We have devolved power to Scotland and to Wales. We are putting in place new agencies to deliver real economic development in our regions. We have started on putting local government back in touch with the people whom it serves. Later in the Session, we shall at long last start to remove the hereditary principle from our system of governance.'[1]

Prescott's speech would not have been out of place in *Alice Through the Looking Glass*.

Illusionary powers of the London Assembly

London Assembly members have no power: it is all make believe.

Members of the Assembly are said to have 'a guiding role'. They debate. They write reports. They can send them to the Mayor. If the Mayor chooses to ignore them he can and does. If two thirds of the Assembly oppose the Mayor's budget they can throw it out. But the Mayor can reintroduce it.

The complex electoral system cannot engage the electorate. London's boroughs are now grouped into 14 large constituencies. Voting for the Assembly is both by party and by candidates. This is said to produce a distribution of seats proportional to the total votes cast across London.

The ballot papers are like a complex examination question with two votes for a mayor and two votes for Assembly Members, one for the constituency and one for London.

What is certain is that elected Assembly members have no real power, so why should voters bother to vote?

The party machine in Scotland and Wales

After several years of so-called devolution there is no feeling of a resurgence of either Scottish or Welsh power.

In Scotland, debate about the success of devolution is acrimonious. Those against say it has not delivered power to electors but has given a stranglehold to a parochial elite of Labour apparatchiks too incompetent to win election to Westminster. Patronage, not independence, is the route to advancement.

In Wales, anger grows as people realise that the Assembly was the product of clever Labour manipulation, and without a clear and unequivocal mandate. Bureaucracy has increased exponentially, while at the same time public services are deteriorating.

Devolution means party machine politics: party managers

vet every candidate. Without sponsorship from the Labour Party in Scotland and Wales it is hard to win office. Labour's nominees pack every quango, grab salaries, cars and expense accounts. A party incapable of winning 50 per cent of the vote exercises 90 per cent of the power. Even supporters have described the Scottish Executive as a place where failed councillors go to die.

Who benefits? The answer in Scotland and Wales is that narrow sectional interest culled from the corrupt culture of single-party local councils. Low-grade career politicians fight for position and wrangle over the fantastic cost of the new parliament buildings.

South of the border there is a hazy impression that Scotland has prospered under devolution. Though it is not politically correct to say so, the Scottish economy lags behind the growth in England. Business failures are alarmingly high.

The single 'upside' of a devolved administration in Scotland and Wales is generous Treasury financing, courtesy largely of the English taxpayer. The downside will be increasing resentment from those same taxpayers.

Elected, unelected, it's all the same

Like London, Scotland and Wales, Assembly members in the eight new English regions are powerless.

Elections will make no difference: they will remain powerless.

One regional assembly member wrote to the author,

> 'Members receive their massive papers only days before the Assembly meets and they have no real idea of what is happening. Only the dedicated few who drive this entire process know. It is a charade of democracy.

'There is a profound sense of Them and Us, the State and the People and a sense of helplessness. In debate members are depressed and unenthusiastic, simply going through the motions. They appear to have no real interest in what they are doing, perhaps because they know they have no power.

'In contrast the Assembly officers are overwhelmingly confident, powerful and consummately professional. They are the real power brokers in stark contrast to the members. The officers seem to enjoy being a small part of a large machine.'[2]

Why bother to vote?

CHAPTER 12

Stakeholders Diminish Democracy

Vested interests inside the assemblies

The concept of 'unelected stakeholders' is foreign to Britain. Stakeholders are the antithesis of democracy. But these petitioners or lobbyists are built into the structure of regional assemblies. These *Social and Economic Partners* represent business, trades unions, religions, charities and environmental groups.

A network of *Economic Partnerships* across the country acts for an array of local organisations including councils, health trusts, universities, and government quangos. For example, the East of England Regional Assembly is part of no less than 173 partnerships. The taxpayer pays for it all.[1]

Add in the CBI, the TUC, ethnic minorities, the UK Youth Parliament (for those aged between 11 and 18 and too young to vote but not too young for the Assemblies), Help the Aged representing similar charities, to name a few.

So diffuse is the partnership structure that one group can be represented in an assembly through several different organisations. It is a cats' cradle.

Because there are not enough seats for the many lobbyists clamouring to be included, new organisations, at even more

expense, represent a motley collection of groups simply to produce a single member to 'represent' them.

For example, to satisfy the many religions or none, there is
a single seat in each regional assembly for what are now called
the Faith Communities. Every region now has Council of
Faiths to represent Christians, Jews, Buddhists, Bahais,
Muslims, Sikhs, Hindus, Druids and Pagans. One man represents all of them in the assembly. And because not all
Christians are happy with such an extraordinary system, in
one or two regions there is one seat for Christians and an extra
seat for Other Faiths (e.g. the East Midlands Regional
Assembly).

In the South East Regional Assembly, the Royal Society for
the Protection of Birds (RSPB) represents all groups involved
with the environment, like the Council for the Protection of
Rural England, regardless of widely differing concerns. Their
new umbrella organisation is the South East Forum for
Sustainability (SEFS).

To say these are vested interests almost understates the
potential for self-serving or worse. Regional assemblies already
have some responsibility for planning. The CBI, sitting in the
Assembly, represents *inter alia* large construction companies.
Those companies will no doubt expect that their interests be
represented on planning issues.

Where does all that leave the man in the street with his one
vote for a local councillor, a councillor who may never be
appointed even to the outer reaches of a regional assembly?

The man in the street is effectively disenfranchised.

The number of lobby groups *inside* assemblies has caused an
explosion of lobby groups *outside* the assemblies, like suppli-
cants round a court. In the case of religion, not only are there
the Councils of Faiths, but most religions now have dedicated
groups to service their interests on the assemblies. The

Churches Regional Network (CRN) co-ordinates Christians in the regions. It pays Regional Officers.

When and if the assemblies are elected, lobbyists cannot be seen to be seated, or even worse voting, in the assembly chamber. That would be an affront to the pretence of democracy. The government is clear about that.

Instead it proposes an underhand solution. The unelected lobbyists may be co-opted onto scrutiny committees, probably with voting rights, and onto policy development committees. They too will be paid.

So unelected lobbyists, largely self-appointed, and paid by the taxpayer will operate behind closed doors on behalf of minority sections of society.

It is a travesty of democracy, but this is the *post democratic society* of the EU.

A Tower of Babel: the quango explosion

Quangos are a growth industry particularly under Labour governments. Regional government has added to that growth exponentially. Many of those running quangos are part of a new class, the bureaucrat mainly owing his livelihood to his political party. Quangos (or more formally Non Departmental Public Bodies) are paid for by the taxpayer and they supposedly act at arms length from the government, which appoints them.

Until recently, these public bodies were few in number, nonpolitical and not contentious. The Trinity House Lighthouse Service appears to have been the first quango established in 1514, followed over the next 400 years by numbers of museums and art galleries like the British Museum in 1753 and the Tate Gallery in 1897.[2]

Today most quangos have a political agenda set by the government, but crucially they are outside all democratic control. That lack of democracy, plus lack of accountability and the abuse of patronage are charges frequently levelled against quangos from all parts of the political spectrum. Parliamentary investigations, think tank and private reports over the last 25 years have highlighted considerable concerns, with over 30 of those reports currently in print.

Still quangos multiply because they strengthen the political influence of the government of the day. There are over 800 quangos in the UK of which over 600 are either executive or advisory.[3] Around the periphery of the British regional assemblies and regional development agencies there are already more than 50 new quangos, to 'assist' the assemblies, all costly with salaried staff.

For example, the Regional Observatory of the West Midlands Regional Development Agency has a director with a salary of £60,000 a year and a staff of 10. Such Observatories monitor the Regional Development Agencies and are repeated across all the regions of the European Union.

The Black Country and East Midlands Observatories have many 'partners'. Here is the description of just one partner. Jargon dominates: presumably *2wm* stands for 2 West Midlands:

> 2wm is a regional site developed in partnership with the Regional Development Agency (AWM), BT, Coventry University and the European Commission. This site is a useful gateway into the West Midlands, from links to business support, land and property searches, jobs, grants, news and events.[4]

Every region has a cultural quango, for example Culture Northeast and Living East, advisory bodies established by the Department for Culture, Media and Sport in 1999 with part-time paid boards of 12 to 20 directors plus full time staff.[5]

Every region has a Small Business Service, a Learning and Skills Council (run on a 'sub-regional basis'), a Housing

Corporation, a Commission of the Arts Council of England, a Public Health Observatory, a Rural Development Service, and a Rural Affairs Forum. All of them receive EU funds.

All of them are in part branches of the EU in Brussels.

Even the quangos are confused over who does what, as the government admitted in its White Paper *Your Region, Your Choice.* Just to talk to each other, the East Midlands Region has to have a 'concordat' with the Regional Development Agency, the Government Office and the Local Government Association.

And on top of all that the salary bill for the regional quangos alone is over £25 million ($45m) every year.

Even National Parks destroy democracy

While National Parks may seem benign, they now have a hidden purpose. Representatives of the Parks sit in the regional

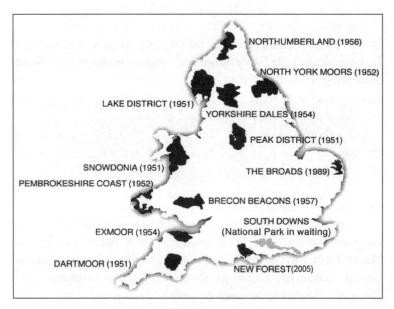

English and Welsh National Parks

assemblies. That is yet another way that the EU is taking over planning.

There are now 15 National Parks covering nearly 15 per cent of the land of England and Wales and about 10 per cent in Scotland. One more is designated, the South Downs.[6]

Although nearly all National Park land is privately owned, yet the way it can be used is now subject to labyrinthine controls. For example, the new South Downs National Park of 632 square miles is heavily populated. Planning powers are to be removed from all constituent towns, like Lewes, and handed to the Park Authority. Just over half the National Park Authority are councillors from across the Park and one-third are *unelected* 'stakeholders' appointed by the government. In turn, just one person will represent the Park Authority in the South East Regional Assembly.

The voters of Lewes, electing a local council to represent their interests in such vital issues as local planning, are denied democracy.

The EU will ultimately control what the people of Lewes can or cannot do with their land and houses through the South East Regional Assembly. Councillors from Chichester to Eastbourne will vote on local Lewes issues, so too will *unelected* national lobby groups.

For a thousand years the New Forest was self-governing, but no longer. Now it is a National Park with its local affairs dictated by outside interests and ultimately by the EU.

The source of all stakeholders

From the start, 'stakeholders' or lobbyists were built into the structure of the EEC. The Economic and Social Committee (ECOSOC), advisory group to the appointed EU Commission set up under the treaty of Rome, has representatives from economic organisations only.

Among the very early proponents of lobbyists or stakeholders

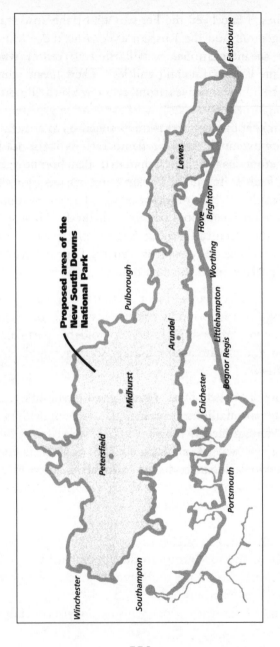

Proposed South Downs National Park

in the 1940s had been the French, led by the academic Denis de Rougemont and the Russian exile, Alexandre Marc. They wanted an international organisation to reflect what they called 'pre-existing social realities'. They meant that there should be representatives from every walk of life and every class.

The stakeholder concept attracts socialists as a useful way of controlling what should be a democratic process: not surprising therefore that its appeal has extended beyond France. In Britain, Federal Trust, the Fabian front organisation, has promoted it.[7]

Yet Federal Trust noted that as 'stakeholders' rose in importance so the electoral turnout has fallen especially from the 1997 general election onwards. Federal Trust believed that the Labour party wanted to show that

> 'it had moved beyond its traditional emphasis on the public sector. Britain's problems were to be tackled through partnership, and 'stakeholders', particularly from the private and voluntary sectors would be the partners.'[8]

The list of 'stakeholders' covers private, voluntary, community, faith, social and environmental. Local councillors are just stakeholders in the assembly.

So this is a way of imposing socialist control. It diminishes the individual elector and that must be an important reason why voters do not vote. It is all part of the *post-democratic society*.

CHAPTER 13

Sub Regions 'Respond to a Strong Regional Voice'

A quiet revolution and the end of counties

Local authorities are now called sub regions. So far, changes to local authorities have been limited and largely related to local planning. But according to John Prescott's *The Future of Local Government: Developing a Ten Year Vision* that situation is about to change.[1] It is hard to imagine a more opaque document, or to discern the true meaning from the jumble of words, with *partnerships* and *targets* repeatedly punctuating its 20 pages.

What is clear is that the Labour government has started a revolution that will eventually overwhelm all local authorities and turn them into representatives of the regions, not of the people. In the words of this first document on the subject, local authorities now have to respond to 'the emergence of a strong regional voice.'[2]

It is time, says the government, to reorganise the sub regions especially with the 'emergence' of more unitary authorities. The death of county councils is an unspoken part of this reorganisation. Their functions will be parcelled out among the local authorities below, or a lucky few may continue as unitaries like Rutland.

The Future of Local Government includes a comprehensive review of councillors, of their numbers, calibre, training and pay. Almost inevitably, given their ever-increasing role, the part time councillor will become a thing of the past. Professional, paid councillors, fewer in number, fit the same pattern as the inner groups of the regional assemblies.

If the principles in this document come to fruition, a new governing class will soon emerge with uncertain consequences.

Transformed after a thousand years

Just as the discarded Kilbrandon Commission report proposed over thirty years ago, even the parish councils are part of the revolution (see page 38).

Parish councils have existed in some form for well over a thousand years. The last major change was when William Gladstone piloted the 1894 Local Government Act through the House of Commons to give more people a say, reflecting a higher level of education.

Parish councils have traditionally been below the political parapet: they epitomise practical commonsense. With limited areas of operation and no political agenda, councils are run frugally, every councillor recognising that a tax rise (or precept) can only come out of his own pocket and that of his neighbour. The total expenditure of all town and parish councils in England is tiny by government standards, £260 million a year ($468 m) and £16 million ($28 m) in Wales.

In England and Wales there are 10,000 parish and town councils. The smallest parish has a population of 22; the largest, Weston-super-Mare, nearly 80,000. The average is 5,000 with 10 councillors per parish. Each councillor represents about 500 people, or 200 households.

Labour campaigns to destroy parish councils

In rural areas there is a strong suspicion that the Labour government wants to undermine, and then replace the entire network of parish councils with a new form of governance.

That suspicion is right.

Government supporters are calling for parish councils to be run by political parties. The government wants contested elections for all councils representing more than 4,500 people. The job of a parish councillor today is a labour of love and duty. There is little or no competition for council seats. If the government wants elections, presumably there will be financial rewards to get enough candidates.

The government is pressing for parish councils to increase taxes (the precept) and to 'educate' people to suffer them. In principle, there is nothing to stop a tax of several thousand pounds per household.

Parish councils are now subject to the heavy hand of a Code of Conduct (another EU term), which is administered by Regional Panels of the Standards Board. Note regions and not counties. Councillors must declare investments above £25,000 ($45,000) in any business, which has dealings in the parish; declare hospitality over £25 ($45); and, perhaps what is worse, inform on their colleagues and neighbours.

Independent tribunals decide if a councillor has breached the code. They may impose penalties ranging from public censure to disqualification for up to five years. Every council has a standards committee: a Statutory Instrument came into force in 2001 on appointments and procedures under which those standards committees operate.[3]

Some parish councils have resigned *en masse* at the intrusion into their private affairs in exchange for doing an unpaid job for the good of the local community.

Down with the English, up with the French

Over a two-year period the National Association of Local Councils (NALC) organised conferences round the country for town councillors and parish clerks. The meetings were mere propaganda exercises: speakers frequently discouraged questions or even refused to take them.

Councillors were flattered with the rhetorical question 'Does our country want big government?' The good news continued with government spokesmen saying the parish councils should be made bigger and layers of government above removed.

What was not admitted is that the only layer to go is the county council, to be replaced by the non-democratic regional assemblies and their complex networks of quangos and 'stakeholders'.

French local councils were praised in the road shows as the model for British town and parish councils to follow. One example was of a French council with 600 voters, a budget of £1 million ($1.8 m) and a huge 90 per cent turnout at elections with income from both local taxes and central government. If adopted in the UK this would translate into a tax (precept) of over £3,000 ($5,400) per household, a tantalising sum for parish councillors to administer.

A vast increase in councillors would be needed: in France there is one councillor for every 100 people compared with 500 in the UK. French mayors are full time paid political appointments in contrast to the British unpaid, part-time Parish Council chairmen. Parish councils elsewhere in the EU are responsible for much more than their British counterparts including libraries, housing, refuse, and water.

While in the UK parish councils only exist in rural areas, in France everywhere is parished. The French policy of decentralisation was lauded at the road shows, even though in reality France is a highly centralised state and is strenuously resisting regionalisation and all that goes with it.

The road shows advocated Public Information Points in every parish for EU information, just like the ones in every public library. Again the message is that England has to catch up with France.

'Best Value', the government's yardstick for local authorities, cannot readily be defined but speakers said that the lowest tender for a service no longer has to be accepted. 'Best Value' appears to be a means by which bureaucrats take control.

Parish councils have to use a new jargon: words like *challenge, consultation,* and *collaboration partners.* The more organisations or 'partnerships' involved in a funding application, the more likely it is to be successful. Road show speakers presented a bewildering array of grant issuing bodies and initiatives with complex organisational charts. There is plenty of money available for those who complete applications with the correct jargon. Speakers were explicit that unless the right framework is used there will be no money. Government brochures showed recalcitrant councillors the right phraseology.

The EU idea of 'partnerships' is promoted even for the bus service. But partnerships defuse criticism from others. No one knows who is responsible or whom to blame. Partnerships dilute accountability and democracy.

In British government language all this simply and benignly reads,

'We will also strengthen the most local tier of administration, the town or parish council, and give it a bigger role. Quality councils which meet certain criteria, including being well managed and good at representing local views, will be able to work more closely with partner authorities to take on more responsibility for shaping their area's development and running its services.'[4]

Neighbourhood councils, 'the heart of new localism'
Early in 2004 the National Association of Local Councils (NALC) put out this statement:

> 'The NALC welcomes a radical review of local community empowerment . . . We welcome too the increasingly positive attitude of principal authorities towards strengthening service delivery at the democratic neighbourhood level. It is vital that this debate is based not on protecting institutions, but rather on looking at the best way of delivering local services in a coherent, holistic and democratic manner.

> 'It is equally vital that local government works much more in partnership with local community and voluntary organisations. This partnership needs to focus on the devolution of decision-making down to the most local level possible. NALC welcomes debate on the creation of new neighbourhood councils. The existing 10,000 community, parish and town councils in England and Wales will be at the heart of new localism: they are the closest tier of local community democracy to residents; and they have a track record of providing excellent service delivery in areas like community safety, environmental services and socio-economic regeneration, as recognised in the recent County Councils' Network report on building community culture.'

The stage is now set for the end of parish councils and their replacement by paid, French-style councils, controlled by one person with an inner group, just like the regional assemblies.

And everyone will pay very dearly for it.

CHAPTER 14

New Regions Envelop Europe

Who defines regions?

People the world over have a strong sense of belonging. In Germany it is called heimat and no German government would dream of interfering with that. In Britain the army's successful regimental system was built on local loyalties.

Yet in a triumph of hope over experience, the British government holds 'that it is not necessary for a region to have a strong historic identity in order to create a modern one.' While the boundaries will 'generate a good deal of fervour' no one will be able to come up with better ones so the 'standard regional boundaries are the right ones.'[1]

That begs the question of whose 'standard' regional boundaries.

Eurostat in Luxembourg, the EU's statistical office, first set up in 1952 to service the European Coal and Steel Commission, defines all regional boundaries. They are not designated in the member states.

Eurostat defines regions as

> 'the expression of a political will; their limits are fixed according to the tasks allocated to the territorial communities, according to the sizes of population

necessary to carry out these tasks efficiently and economically, and according to historical, cultural and other factors.'[2]

What are cumbersomely called 'uniform geographical units' or 'normative regions' were used in 1961 at that first Brussels' regional economic conference. Since 1988 they have been used in Community legislation.

Population decrees

In 2003, the EU issued a regulation enforcing the regional system. The excuse was the EU's enlargement from 15 to 25 countries. Today every country must have EU regions.[3] The EU has over 130 regions; beneath them are sub regions, and sub sub regions. They are also called Nomenclature of Territorial Units for Statistics (NUTS), another unwieldy title translated from the French.[4]

By EU decree in 2003 the size of each region is defined by population:

Level	NUTS	Minimum	Maximum
Region	NUTS 1	3 million	7 million
Sub region	NUTS 2	800,000	3 million
Sub sub region	NUTS 3	150,000	800,000

In 2005, the Commission will publish a report on imposing a fourth level with even smaller populations called Local Administrative Units (LAU). These embrace districts and municipalities and they are numbered in Brussels down to ward level of less than 10,000 voters.

The City of London just a neighbourhood council

Only the regions of London, Yorkshire, Scotland, Wales and Northern Ireland have borders, which are roughly the same as old UK boundaries. Some of the new regions are a very odd shape, making no sense at all.

The Southeast region looks like a sandwich from which a bite-sized chunk has been removed. It goes south from Milton Keynes in Bedfordshire via Berkshire, Hampshire and then swings east to encompass the whole of Kent, Surrey and Sussex leaving a large hole for London. None of these counties has been united before and from whatever angle the region is addressed it is a nonsense.

Without the slightest pretence of democratic legitimacy, in 2004 planning committees of the English regional assemblies' followed Brussels' orders and carved up their own regions into sub-regions to fit the Brussels' Spatial Plan for the whole of Europe.

Though most Londoners do not know it, London is now EU region number UK I. But London too has been subdivided.

Anyone checking a planning application will already have discovered that London is divided into an alien system with outer and inner sub-regions numbered UK I 1 and UK I 2. Those sub regions are divided again into five: Inner London West UKI 1 1; Inner London East UKI 1 2; Outer London East and NE, UKI 21; Outer London South UKI 22; and Outer London West and NW, UKI 23.

Ken Livingstone, Mayor of the London Region, plans to abolish all 33 London boroughs and replace them with five super boroughs, neatly fitting this Brussels plan. It will mean the end of well-known boroughs like the Royal Borough of Kensington and Chelsea, Westminster and the City of London. All will be reduced to sub sub regions called Neighbourhood Councils, the new word for the parish councils.

No doubt there are shocks in store for all parts of England and in particular for all county councils. Devon County Council, for example, is already reduced to a sub sub region of the EU, UKK 43, and Dorset County Council UKK 22, pending their abolition.

That will be the end of hundreds of years of successful British local government and of local identity. The County of Kent is the UK's oldest administrative unit, already in existence with roughly today's boundaries when Julius Caesar first arrived in 55 BC and, so says its motto *Invicta*, unconquered, though the Romans and Normans might have questioned that.

All change, except in Germany

> 'A remarkable process of devolution has been playing out in most member states over the last few decades. Centralised states such as France, Belgium and the United Kingdom have become decentralised or federal states . . . Regions, towns and localities have in the meantime become the bedrock of the European system of government . . .'
>
> *Jos Chabert, President of the Committee of the Regions, September 2001*

M. Chabert has wildly overstated his case. But as they are legally required to do, all the EU countries are changing to the EU system, often painfully and expensively like the UK.

If anyone has doubts as to the provenance of regionalisation, they would do well to study this view from Brussels. The EU's Committee of the Regions once helpfully published a series of charts showing the progress of each towards total devolution.[5] The charts are no longer available, perhaps because they so clearly signalled the EU takeover of local government.

The most recent applicants, the countries of Eastern Europe, were required to change their local government before joining the EU. For example, in January 1999 Poland adopted the EU's three-tier system of government, replacing its 49 provinces or voivodships with 16 regions. Because many of the 49 voivodships had only been created in 1975, they were not much lamented.[6] Each new region has a directly elected parliament, as yet without tax raising or legislative powers, and a centrally appointed governor representing the prime minister.

Not surprisingly, in most of the countries which had joined the EU earlier, there is resistance to the abolition of centuries old boundaries and allegiances. Change is proceeding slowly. Each country is at a different stage on the road to the EU system. These governments do not make a direct link for their voters between the upheaval in local government and membership of the EU.

Germany is the one exception to this upheaval. The 16 German Länder appear to be blueprints for EU local government. Each Länder has its own constitution, parliament and executive and judiciary plus tax raising powers. Members are elected by the EU approved Additional Member System.

The only major change in Germany has been the revision of the Basic Law in 1992 after the reunification of Germany to give the Länder a greater role in EU affairs, independently of the German government. Under article 23 of the German Constitution, if a Land already has the power, it must be allowed to take part in forming the German government's opinion on Europe. In some cases, this means being able to negotiate with the EU.

The Länder and the German government have since fallen out about who should do what at the European level. In 2004, the federal government resisted demands by the heads of Länder for more power at the EU level. As a result, the federal government set up a special commission to resolve the issue, jointly chaired by Franz Müntefering, the head of the governing SPD, and Edmund Stoiber, the head of the opposition conservative CSU.

France threatened with break-up

France is the most centralised country in Europe and faces the biggest upheaval.

Although a referendum in 1969 rejected regionalisation, only three years later regional bodies with some economic responsibility were set up. In response to constant cajoling from Brussels, in 1982 President François Mitterand created 22 regions with limited powers under the Deferre Act. The new *conseils regionaux* cannot legislate. In 1986 Mitterand held the first elections.

In 2002 President Jacques Chirac campaigned on decentralisation. He called it 'un formidable levier pour enfin réformer l'Etat'. He assured electors that the first article of the French constitution, France is 'a single and indivisible republic', was sacrosanct. He was not seeking a federal state.

Crucially, at no time has this issue been presented in France in this context as a EU issue: it is simply a matter for France.

The campaign to introduce what the French call *girondisme* is highly controversial.[7] *Girondisme* is a U turn: it rejects the way France has been governed since the French Revolution when the Jacobins defeated the Girondins and imposed central power.

If the central power of Paris is destroyed and the 96 départements abolished in favour of the 22 EU regions, then the French map will return to about the year 1,000 AD.

In March 2003 the French Constitution was changed to devolve power to regions and departments over economic development, transport, tourism, culture and further education. Provision was also made for local referendums. In July 2003 Corsica held a referendum and narrowly voted No to an assembly with limited powers to raise and spend taxes.

More snapshots of a changing Europe

○ Austria has Länder but they are weaker than the German Länder and have yet to be strengthened. Their authority only covers planning, law, agriculture, youth, theatre, sport and tourism. In 1988, the Länder gained the power to agree international treaties.

○ Belgium was formed in 1831 as a centralised, single language state on the French model. The French diplomat Talleyrand[8] described it as 'an artificial construction, consisting of different peoples'. Belgium was reconstituted in federal form in 1993. Its 'co-operative federalism' embraces three language communities (French, German and Flemish), and three economic regions (Brussels, Flanders, Walloon). Belgian laws enacting Council of Europe charters for the protection of minorities have given the German-speaking minority political scope to increase its autonomy. Even secession from the Belgian state is no longer excluded from debate, though strongly opposed by the Walloon region. The German minority lives in the former Reich districts of Eupen and Malmedy, transferred to Belgium under the 1919 Treaty of Paris (Versailles).

○ Finland created 19 regional councils of limited powers in 1994 expressly to get EU grants.

○ Greece, six years before it joined the EU in 1981, created 13 development regions with no significant powers as yet.

○ Ireland in 1994 created eight regional authorities and in 1999 two regional assemblies with limited powers.

○ In Italy the regions have limited powers. The 20 'regioni' (five special, 15 ordinary) have no tax raising powers; members are elected every five years by a list system with responsibility for health, welfare, town planning, tourism, culture and agriculture.

○ The Netherlands has 12 provinces with responsibility for

traffic, public transport, town planning and the environment. They do not yet have legislative powers, and raise revenue only through motor vehicle tax.

o The Portuguese voted against 'self-governing' regions in a 1998 referendum. Despite the No vote, the following year regional development agencies were *imposed* on the Portuguese. They are unelected so-called partnerships of local lobby groups, just like the Regional Development Agencies in England. The islands of the Azores and Madeira have a form of autonomy.

o In the late 1970s, after the death of Franco, 17 Spanish regions were created but most of them like Navarre had existed for many hundreds of years before Franco. Each *communidades autonomic* has its own president, executive, parliament and high court of justice. Some have more powers (e.g. tax systems, police) than the standard portfolio of education, health, urban planning, culture, agriculture and social services.

o Sweden's regionalisation is proceeding haphazardly. Some regions have been created for different purposes but in doing so the Swedish Regional Commission (Region-beredningen) failed to take account of the EU system. The southern part of Sweden has two new regional divisions: one for the EU and one for domestic purposes. The new regions do not match historical boundaries, many of which date back many hundreds of years. Scania's borders date to 380 AD.

Too small to have a future?

What will happen to the small states and islands in Europe, which do not meet the EU's population criteria to be a region? Estonia and Latvia, currently nation states, fall into the sub-region category, Luxembourg is technically a sub sub region. But many are too small even to be sub sub regions.

Probably in time all will be combined with neighbouring regions and certainly not the nation state with which historically they have been most closely linked. Local loyalties must be broken.

In the case of British dependencies and territories:

○ The Isle of Man with its parliament dating back to the Vikings will be part of Northern Ireland, even though it is as yet outside the EU

○ The Channel Islands after a thousand years under the Duke of Normandy (the Queen) will join Normandy, though again they are outside the EU

○ Gibraltar with Spain

○ Malta with Italy

Will Cyprus be part of a Greek or a Turkish region?

The independent countries and principalities of Monaco, Andorra, Liechtenstein and Luxembourg will be absorbed into the regions of neighbouring countries: Germany, France and Spain.

An integrated Europe of regions and cities indeed!

CHAPTER 15

The EU Spins across a Continent

From the Atlantic to Vladivostock

The British government has repeatedly stated that the creation of British regions is entirely a domestic affair. The office of the European Commission in London reiterates that British regions have no connection with Brussels at all; any such suggestions are a myth.

All the evidence is to the contrary and the fact that regions are being introduced across the EU, including those countries applying to join the EU, confirms that they are not a British invention for a purely British purpose. The 12 'British' regions are part of a revolution in 'local' government across Europe.

Indeed, the crusade to create an integrated European Union of the regions and the cities was never limited to the original six countries, the nine, the 15 or now the 25. Planning embraces the whole of Europe, from the Atlantic to the Urals. Russia is in the Council of Europe, the 'waiting room' of the EU, so it may be more apposite to write from the Atlantic to Vladivostock.

As countries join the EU, so they have to regionalise their government structure, as the treaty of Rome and the acquis communautaire require. The next stage is to give those regions more and more power at the expense of the nation states but to ensure that those powers are virtually meaningless.

If present plans come to fruition, the result might well be one centralised state covering the whole of Europe, even extending into Asia.

Lobby groups junket across Europe

To promote regional government and more power for the regions across Europe, the EU Commission has created groups to lobby itself, and to create a cacophony of support. The EU Constitutional Convention involved five of these lobby groups to craft a 'dialogue with civil society' on the text of the EU Constitution.

The Commission financed every single one of them with tax-payers' money. There was nothing independent about it.

The British government has imitated the EU. It has lobbied itself on regional government using groups it pays to do the job: the English Regions Network, the LGIU, the Constitutional Conventions and the CFER (see pages 66).

Both the Commission and the British government try to give the impression of a wide-ranging debate with independent groups. Yet it is a charade. There is no dialogue, only propaganda.

The EU's lobby groups are an alphabet soup of sycophants: CoR, ECOSOC, CALRE, REGLEG, AEBR, CEMR, AER, CRPM. And those are just the better known ones.

British and indeed Europe's taxpayers fund thousands of officials and part time 'representatives' on large expense accounts, meeting regularly, usually in the sunnier parts of Europe. This is junketing on a continental scale.

Typical of the EU lobby groups is the Committee of the Regions (CoR).[1] Inserted into the Maastricht Treaty 'at the request of the German Länder ', the CoR has no power whatsoever in a 'government' where the Commission initiates and develops all policies. It is there to advise the Commission.

Although it is just a talking shop, the EU promotes the CoR as a key to governance. It 'represents' 85,000 local and regional authorities. It gives 'Opinions'. It is 'consulted'.

Any thought that the CoR gives any democratic representation to EU regions is false. CoR members may *only* act in the interests of the EU, not their regions, nor their countries.

The CoR complements that other group of placemen, the Economic and Social Committee (ECOSOC), which dates back to the treaty of Rome of 1957. The two groups are identical in structure. While the CoR draws its membership from the regions, ECOSOC is based on economic organisations. With 317 people each, they are very unwieldy.

The UK contributes 24 members to the Committee of the Regions, two for each region including Scotland, Wales and Northern Ireland. If in due course regional assemblies are elected in England, they will then nominate members of the CoR, a role they currently share with the Local Government Association (LGA). The Scottish and Welsh members are nominated by their regional assemblies, the Scottish Parliament and the National Assembly for Wales.

The real task of the CoR is to act as a channel of communication between Brussels and the regions to ensure that local officials comply with the Commission. Officials are paid for their loyalty to Brussels.

Even the last CoR's president admitted that the CoR does not enjoy a good reputation with 'marginal' effectiveness.[2] Birmingham councillors attacked their City Council leader, Sir Albert Bore, for splitting his time between a EU appointed group and the affairs of Birmingham. He insisted that as president of the CoR he brought more EU money to Birmingham for regeneration projects. After his term as president, Sir Albert stayed on as the CoR's vice president.

Endemic corruption

The CoR, an organisation with no responsibilities, has been plagued by corruption and scandal as some members add to their private bank balances. A brave whistleblower brought that endemic corruption to light.

Over a three-year period its internal auditor, Robert McCoy, investigated the CoR's budget of £27 million ($48.6m) a year. He discovered serious irregularities in expense claims from the CoR's members, who travel from all round the EU to meetings in Brussels at least six times a year. He asked the CoR's permanent Secretary General, Vincenzo Falcone, to report the cases to the EU's anti-fraud office, OLAF. Falcone refused. Colleagues cold-shouldered McCoy for asking 'inappropriate' questions and a senior official threatened him with disciplinary action.

So McCoy audited the expenses himself and found a mountain of fraud. CoR members had claimed for travel without proof, some for mileage allowances totalling hundreds of euros for journeys already paid by their cities or councils. Others had fictional meetings to claim a daily allowance of £144 ($260). More claimed for business-class plane tickets but travelled on a cut-price airline and pocketed the difference. The 'profit' could be hundreds of euros.

Yet Falcone, the Secretary General of the CoR, ordered McCoy to stop investigating.

Then McCoy discovered possible fraud in two outside printing contracts. Again Falcone did not want the anti-fraud office involved. Other officials tried to persuade McCoy to turn a blind eye. Instead he took his findings to the Secretary General, Sir Albert Bore. Even he ordered that the contracts should go ahead. In frustration, McCoy gave details to a MEP.

So early in 2003, MEPs refused to approve the CoR's 2001 accounts, freezing a quarter of its 2004 budget and inviting McCoy to answer questions. Within days, the MEPs summoned both the anti-fraud office (OLAF) and the European Court of Auditors to investigate. The Court of Auditors agreed that the problems were genuine, but declared no 'substantial infringement' of the rules.

OLAF confirmed the fraud. Its report accused the CoR of an 'endemic culture of unprofessionalism and improvisation 'where intransparency is preferred above openness'. In all 222 members of staff had made false claims for travel expenses.

As a result, Falcone's appointment was annulled. OLAF recommended Falcone be disciplined but he was given six months unpaid leave, ensuring that he clocked up enough service to receive a full pension.

But in typical EU style the CoR management, no doubt to protect their own pecuniary interests, made McCoy's life so unpleasant that according to Chris Heaton-Harris, the British Conservative MEP,

'Robert is a broken man sitting at home in a deep depression, suffering from recurrent insomnia, nightmares and panic attacks. What a way to end a long career of public service. What sort of message does this sort of thing send out on the way the EU conducts its affairs?'[3]

Regions and the European Court of Justice

'To strengthen and extend regional government in the EU' in 1997 the EU created the Conference of the European Regional Legislative Assemblies (CALRE). Only regions that can pass some of their own laws are members.[4] CALRE works with the CoR and the Council of Europe's Congress of Local and Regional Authorities of Europe.[5] It represents over 60 regional assemblies across Europe, but none are in France because French regions have no legislative power.

Members include:

o Scottish Parliament

○ National Assembly for Wales
○ 19 parliaments of the Spanish autonomous communities
○ 21 Italian regional councils
○ 5 Belgian Chambers of the Regions and Communities
○ 9 Austrian parliaments of the Länder
○ 16 German parliaments of the Länder
○ Åland Islands parliament (Finland)
○ Azores and Madeira regional assemblies

In September 2003, CALRE's Italian President, Riccardo Nencini of the region of Tuscany, led the First Ministers of Scotland and Wales with the other 195 presidents and vice presidents of regional assemblies in Europe, in approving the *Charter of European Regions: Crossing Borders*. The regional presidents demanded that the EU should recognise 'the fundamental role of European regional assemblies for European integration', and their right to bring actions directly to the European Court of Justice, so bypassing nation states.

In July 2004, all the regional presidents issued what they called the Declaration of Arnhem demanding

> 'a clear role for the regional assemblies contributing to the development of regional democracy and regionalism throughout the European continent, in the framework of a process of integration and enlargement, with increasing contact with new neighbours and strives towards an active role for assemblies in the process of policy-making . . . The conference confirms the vital role of cross border, interregional and transborder co-operation for the future of Europe and asks the European Union and the Member States to facilitate this cooperation on a European scale.'[6]

At its Intergovernmental Conference (IGC) in 2000 the EU

created another lobby group expressly to promote regions. It is almost identical to CALRE but has no formal role with the EU institutions. The Conference of European Regions With Legislative Power (REGLEG) with 64 members was another part of the paid chorus to ensure that 'regions with legislative powers' were recognised the following year in the Laeken Declaration on the future of the EU.[7]

In November 2003, Jack McConnell, Scotland's First Minister and the chairman of REGLEG, demanded direct Scottish access to the European Court of Justice in Luxembourg, which would mean bypassing the British court system. Under McConnell's chairmanship, REGLEG expressed strong concern that the proposed EU constitution did not entitle their regions to 'refer directly to the European Court of Justice when their prerogatives are harmed or other actors exceed their competences'.

The role of the Council of Europe

The ultimate lobby group is the Council of Europe. The Commission uses the Council of Europe to expand its influence and its power. Although legally separate, the Council of Europe and the EU are mutually supportive. Their links are evoked by the Council of Europe's logo of the EU's ring of gold stars on a blue background with an overlay of the letter C. The Council of Europe has the declared aim of 'greater unity between its members', almost identical to the EU's aim of political union.[8]

The Council of Europe, known as the waiting room for the EU, acts as the advance guard to draw countries inside the EU. Grants are used as bribes. Council of Europe Conventions (or agreements) often migrate into EU legislation where they have much more force. For example, the European Social Charter and the European Charter on Human Rights were both first introduced as Council of Europe conventions.

CALRE and REGLEG come under the auspices of the Council of Europe and not the EU. They can therefore include countries currently outside the EU but which might hope to join.

CALRE and REGLEG are indicative of the many groups created to ululate their support for the EU's agenda of political integration. In return these hundreds of individuals are sated with the perks of regular expenses-paid meetings all over Europe, courtesy of the taxpayer.

The other main groups are:

1 Association of European Border Regions (AEBR) sited in Gronau, Germany promotes the *European Charter of Border and Cross-Border Regions*. 90 border and cross-border regions are members. The title of its newsletter makes its intent clear, *Partnership in a Europe without Borders*. No UK border region is yet a member.

2 Council of European Municipalities and Regions (CEMR), founded 1951, works for a united Europe of self-governing regions with a membership of over 100,000 towns and regions. It has two headquarters are in Brussels and Paris. The Local Government International Bureau leads the British contingent.

3 Assembly of European Regions (AER) was created in 1985 to unite the regions of Europe in an integrated Europe. Based in Strasbourg, it includes 250 Regions from 30 countries and 12 interregional organisations. British members are the counties of Devon, Dorset, Fife, Gloucestershire, Hampshire, Somerset, and West Sussex and the West Midlands region

4 Conference of Peripheral Maritime Regions of Europe (CRPM) promotes regional planning in 149 European coastal regions from 27 countries. 19 of them are British.[9] It is based in Rennes in France.

5 Eurocities with its HQ in Brussels is a Europe-wide association of 85 large cities, including 15 from the UK: Belfast, Birmingham, Bradford, Bristol, Cardiff, Edinburgh, Glasgow, Kingston upon Hull, Leeds, Liverpool, Manchester, Newcastle/Gateshead, Nottingham, Sheffield and Southampton. Manchester currently holds the presidency.

CHAPTER 16

'Borders are the Scars of History'

Border Regions in Britain

The place names Transmanche and Région Rives-Manche probably mean little or nothing to most people in the UK. Most maps do not show them. So where or what are they?

The British may be surprised to learn that Transmanche and Région Rives-Manche are two British regions, or, to be more accurate, partly British. Neither has a name in English and information about them is mainly in French. Even odder, both regions span the English Channel as though it were a stream.

Transmanche and Région Rives-Manche are Border Regions, also known as Euroregions or Euregios. As the names imply each encompasses a national border and is based on the slim premise that areas around national borders are severely economically deprived and need special treatment. People living in counties along the south coast of England would not recognise that they are a Border Region, or severely economically deprived or united with France.

Across the continent of Europe there are now over 70 Border Regions uniting over 200 regions or, in the British case, counties. All are large with several million inhabitants, and all take in parts of at least two countries. They already include about half the EU land mass and a third of its population.

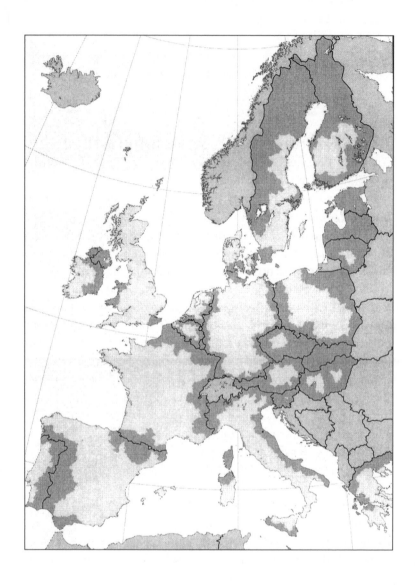

Border Regions across the EU

Transmanche includes the English county of Kent, and regions in France and Belgium. According to the Transmanche web site 'taking advantage of the Channel Tunnel', Kent County Council and the Regional Council of Nord-Pas-De-Calais in France signed a co-operation agreement in 1987 to be funded by the EU's Interreg programme. In 1991 that agreement was extended to Brussels, Flanders and Wallonia in Belgium.

Similarly, the Région Rives-Manche combines the English county of East Sussex with the Seine-Maritime and the Somme across the Channel in France.

Both the East Sussex and Kent County Councils view these Border Regions purely in terms of obtaining more money for their voters in EU grants. Since 1992 those grants have been worth more than £26 million ($46 m) to Kent alone. Under the EU's Interreg IIIA programme, £70 million ($126 m) is available for the authorities on both sides of the Channel, another £61 million ($109 m) from national and regional budgets and £22 million ($40 m) from private funding, totalling £153 million ($275 m).

The EU puts a different interpretation on the projects.

'The Channel simultaneously divides and joins two parts of Western Europe, which for centuries have shared common events to create a joint History. A thousand year period, beginning with the Norman invasion of England, now nears its end as that same island becomes physically linked to the continent of Europe.'[1]

Neither Kent nor East Sussex is allowed to be part of the management of 'their' Border Regions. The French Regional Council of Upper Normandy in Rouen manages both of them. In the UK the Government Office of the Southeast (GOSE) is the corresponding party.

Essex partnership with Thüringen, Germany and Picardy, France

Other English counties have signed agreements with French départements, which are precursors to Border Regions. Essex has an agreement with Nord Pas de Calais, Cornwall with Finisterre, Devon with Calvados, Dorset with Manche and East Sussex with Haute-Normandie.

Hampshire County Council, which describes itself as 'a unique border region in Europe', is in the early stages of creating the UK's third Border Region to include Basse-Normandie, West Sussex and the Isle of Wight.

'Gilbertian' projects across the English Channel

Transmanche and Région Rives-Manche are both classed by the EU as 'emerging' Border Regions, and their activities are at present confined to cultural, educational and tourist projects, regarded in Brussels as easy programmes to carry out.

For example, *The Guardian* of 7 January 2004 carried an advertisement for a manager for an 'Above the Waist' project. Candidates funded by the European Regional Development Fund at £27,514 to £37,466 a year will work in both the Somme in France and Kent on exploring 'young people's values and attitudes to sex, relationships and teenage pregnancy'.

Chatham Dockyards hands out a leaflet, *Maritime Heritage*, financed by the EU Regional Development Fund, to promote 'the Transmanche region's rich maritime cultural heritage'. Helpfully it is written in both English and French, presumably in the belief that a family on a day out would zigzag across the Channel on the Maritime Heritage Trail. The English half of the trail runs from Romney Marsh along the Kent coast to Gravesend; the French along the entire Nord Pas de Calais coastline from Dunkirk to Berck.

Gilbert and Sullivan would perhaps have added these projects to that 'little list . . . they'll none of 'em be missed'.[2]

Challenging British interests in Gibraltar

For many years Spain has laid claim to Gibraltar, a claim that the British government has usually robustly denied, and nearly all Gibraltarians have repeatedly and loudly demonstrated their total antipathy to being part of Spain. So a particularly sensitive Border Region is that of Gibraltar joined with Spanish Andalusia and Morocco in North Africa but only 12 miles across the Straits of Gibraltar. Morocco is of course outside the EU and not, as yet, an applicant country.

Spain too has hostages to this EU increase of influence: Ceuta and Melita are two Spanish enclaves within Morocco, which Morocco claims.

It is not lost on the EU, which funds the Border Region, that

> 'Gibraltar's pivotal position at the entrance to the Mediterranean has historically made it an important strategic bastion'.[3]

Brussels plans a continental union

While the idea of British Border Regions may seem Gilbertian, the inclusion of Gibraltar in the list should start to ring alarm bells. There is a very serious intent to the spread of Border Regions. The EU's stated aim is to create a territorial unit on both sides of a national border and eventually to remove the border 'to improve economic exchange'. The Transmanche web site, for example, admits that this is part of the 'ongoing process of European integration' and the removal of national boundaries.[4]

Border Regions are another joint project between the EU and the Council of Europe: the EU gives most of the money and the Council of Europe provides the legal framework. These huge regions are deliberately designed to include ethnic minorities, preferably those that straddle both sides of a national border, another cause for alarm bells to ring.

National borders and the regions adjacent to them were recognised as particularly important in that second EEC Commission document of 1969 on developing regional policy (see page 22). Since then the Commission has regularly emphasised co-operation across national borders.

Setting up a legal entity to erode national sovereignty has not been straightforward. The first agreements between adjacent regions were effectively twinnings, relying largely on goodwill. Associations were set up within each country and then agreements were made between them across the border. Later, the 1980 Madrid Convention under the auspices of the Council of Europe created a legal framework to develop the Border Regions (see page 181).

As yet, any decisions made by the Border Region authorities are binding only on the public authorities and not on the individuals who live within the regions.

From 1988 onwards when more EU money was available there was a sharp rise in the creation of Border Regions. There were no Border Regions on the Austrian-German border before Austria joined the EU in January 1995, but in the following four years five new Border Regions were started. As countries in Eastern Europe applied to join the EU, so they too were divided into Border Regions.

According to the EU Commission, the Interreg Community Initiative, adopted in 1990, prepared border areas for a Community without internal frontiers. Border Regions are funded to

> 'ensure that national borders are not a barrier to balanced development and the integration of Europe . . .'⁵

The EU's money goes to the whole of Europe, and as far afield as Russia, the Black Sea and North Africa. That money is a sweetener to entice non-members to join the EU and extend its influence. Applicant countries receive Brussels' grants to break down their borders and link into the neighbouring regions of existing EU members.

Switzerland with its substantial banking sector, and Norway with huge resources of oil, are both particular targets for EU's Border Regions. Both are still outside the EU.

The Nordic Council of Ministers from Norway, Sweden, Finland and Denmark receives EU grants for its eight Border Regions.

Switzerland is a key target for EU handouts or bribes and all its borders are part of Border Regions. The EU's Interregional grant is according to its web site 'of direct consequence for Switzerland', because of 'the necessity of integrating Switzerland in European regional planning'. The EU justifies this by talk of 'the mutual influence of the regions of Switzerland and neighbouring countries'; Swiss towns 'belong to a network of European cities' and the Swiss railway is joined to the European network.

Border Regions began in Germany

Border Regions have given rise to extensive research in universities, much of which is EU funded. One such paper claims that Border Regions are

> 'clearly a predominantly German phenomenon . . .
> the Euroregion, understood as an institutional form,
> has been "invented" in Germany and . . . enjoys a
> considerable legitimacy within the federalist German
> system.'[6]

That is indeed the case. Today all Germany's borders are within Border Regions and they are far more integrated than the 'emerging' Border Regions of Transmanche and Région Rives-Manche spanning the English Channel.

In 1958, a year after the Treaty of Rome was signed with its many clauses emphasising regional, not national, economic policy, Germany created the first Border Region. It embraces part of Germany and the Netherlands and over 3 million people. Called EUREGIO, and described on its website as 'a life without borders', it includes the German Länder of North Rhine-Westphalia and Lower Saxony, and three Dutch regions centred on the town of Enschede.

A cross border parliament endorsed by Prince Klaus of the Netherlands was set up in 1979. The EUREGIG council is elected by all the city councils within the Border Region, with its political parties represented in proportion to the results of regional elections.

The EUREGIO's headquarters of 30 German and Dutch staff is in the German town of Gronau, symbolically exactly where the customs checkpoint once stood. In 1992 the European Association of Border Regions moved to a permanent purpose-built home in Gronau, appropriately called 'EUREGIO House' (see page 182).

A 1981 resolution by the first EUREGIO starkly laid out the thinking behind border regions. The resolution said that borders are the 'scars of history' and

> 'border and cross-border regions are therefore components and brides in the European unification process.' Nation states are the problem. Nation states had partitioned ethnic groups in the nineteenth and twentieth centuries. Without the need for defence, there would of course be no need for borders.[7]

The mastermind on the Dutch side of the EUREGIO was not Dutch, as might be assumed, but a German, Alfred Mozer.[8] In March 1933 at the time of the last democratic election in Germany before Hitler took power, Alfred Mozer was the editor of *Der Volksbote*, a regional SPD newspaper in Emden. All Social Democrat newspaper in Germany were then banned, and Mozer, like many other socialists and liberals, was briefly jailed. He fled across the German border to the Netherlands where he continued to be active in both German émigré and Dutch socialist circles throughout the war and later.

Unlike the majority of the Dutch in the 1940s and 1950s, Alfred Mozer was an ardent believer in European integration. He was close to Chancellor Konrad Adenauer, a prime mover in the creation of the EEC backed by the powerful Zentrum Group in the Rhineland.[9] He was also influential with successive Dutch governments. In 1958, the Dutch EEC agricultural commissioner, Sicco Mansholt, asked Mozer to be his private secretary. He was the first International Secretary of the Dutch Labour Party (PvdA). After retiring in 1970, he chaired the Mozer Commission co-ordinating the first Border Region between the Netherlands and Germany.

Integrating the English Channel within the EU

Another variety of Border Region is the Working Community of which there are thirteen across Europe. They are looser associations of regions and the most ambitious involve five or six countries with assemblies of regional heads of governments, a commission of executive officers, a general secretariat, plus standing commissions on a wide range of issues. For example, Alpes-Adria, set up in 1978, includes parts of the countries of Austria, Switzerland, Germany, Italy, Croatia, Slovenia and Hungary – 19 regions in all. Its standing commissions include regional planning, tourism, traffic, the environment, sport, and minorities. Euregio Baltyk, started in 1998, encompasses parts of Poland, Latvia, Lithuania, Sweden, Denmark and Russia.

The only Working Community to include parts of the UK is Arc Manche founded in 1996 with a declaration of intent to integrate the Channel costal regions within the EU. It has not made much progress. On the French side are Brittany, Nord-

Pas de Calais, Lower Normandy, Upper Normandy, Picardy and on the British the counties of Dorset, Hampshire, Kent, West Sussex, East Sussex and the Isle of Wight. Essex, Cornwall and Devon are observers.

There has been one failure: Arc Atlantique, which combined regions bordering the Atlantic from the UK, Spain, France Portugal and Ireland, collapsed in 2004. It was just too ambitious.

Road, rail, energy and water cross borders

Energy is an EU competence or power and the EU is concerned with renewable and cleaner sources of energy, both within the EU and in neighbouring countries. The EU is developing one market, a single market, in gas, oil, coal and electricity to secure the continuity of supplies. That might be sensible enough.

But the EU's energy plan, Regen, goes further. It links regions across national borders with electricity cables and gas pipelines so they become interdependent and no longer self-reliant. The Channels Islands have shut down their coal-fired power station and they are now entirely reliant on electricity delivered via an undersea cable from Normandy in France. That can even create opportunities for blackmail, as Monaco discovered when the French government threatened to switch off its lights if it did not conform on tax.

The EU finances all this through its Interregional or Interreg fund. The second five-year plan from 2000 to 2006, funded with nearly £3.5 billion ($6.5 bn), is divided into three and for the purposes of the *European Spatial Development Perspective* (ESDP) the UK appears in all three categories but each time grouped with different countries:

○ The first, Interreg III A, promotes 'better integration with-in the Union through the formation of large groups of

European regions' and funds Transmanche and the other Border Regions

○ The second, Interreg III B, builds energy networks particularly in the 'ultra-peripheral regions and island regions'. Britain is in the *North Sea region* together with Belgium, Denmark, Germany, the Netherlands, Sweden, and Norway

○ The third, Interreg III C, develops water resources, again within huge regions. Britain is in the *West Zone of Europe* with Belgium, France, Germany, Ireland, Luxembourg, and the Netherlands

The results of all this fulfils the EU's original aim: local and regional authorities are steadily being 'Europeanised'. Border Regions are playing an increasing role in their countries' relationship with the EU. National borders are weakened. Countries are becoming more and more reliant on neighbouring countries for gas, electricity and water supplies.

Are Border Regions *only* a device to hasten the end of the nation state? Might they be ends in themselves? One day will the whole continent of Europe from the Atlantic even to Vladivostock, be organised in these big cross-national groupings thus completely eradicating countries?

And finally, the EU has even divided the whole continent of Europe into twelve huge planning areas, which go well beyond the present EU borders. They are the Alpine Space, Archimed, Atlantic Area, Baltic Area, Central and Danubian Space, the North Sea, the North West European Metropolitan Area (NWMA), the Northern Periphery, Most Remote Regions, Southwest Europe, the Western Mediterranean and lastly Overseas. The UK is but a small part of area NWMA.

CHAPTER 17

Manipulating Minorities to Divide and Rule

Cornwall for the Cornish

After centuries of decline there has recently been a rising interest in the Cornish language and Cornish history. That might pass without much comment were it not for considerable pressure from outside the UK promoting both the language and the Cornish identity which, bizarre though it might seem, if taken to its logical conclusion could even begin to challenge the integrity of the UK as a sovereign state.

In 1999 Bernard Deacon, a lecturer at the relatively new Institute of Cornish Studies, part of the University of Exeter, argued in *A Cornish National Minority Report* that the British government should recognise the Cornish as a separate cultural group and give them minority status. His work was financed by the Joseph Rowntree Reform Trust, the charity that had financed all the British Constitutional Conventions and the Campaign for the English Regions.

Deacon's report concluded that 'the Cornish have a distinct historic identity, with origins that are non-English. There are also a number of constitutional, linguistic and cultural "differences". These elements combine to produce a claim to be regarded as a national minority that fits even the restricted UK

Government definition of the term "national minority".' Deacon sent his report to the Council of Europe to be considered within its Framework Convention for the Protection of National Minorities.

Not long afterwards another group, the Federal Union of European Nationalities (FUEN) based in Germany, argued the same line.[1] Its 2002 congress demanded that the British government should 'recognise the Cornish as a national minority in line with the Framework Convention' and went even further by calling for the revival of the Cornish Stannary Parliament.

The Stannary or tinners' parliament had been set up in the eleventh century to legislate for the thousands of Cornish tin miners working some 350 miles from London and several days journey away who needed fast local justice. It was abandoned in 1752, when the sharply rising profits of overseas tin mines led to the emigration of Cornish miners in large numbers. The Stannary powers have never been rescinded by the British parliament, they just fell into abeyance, and a very few Cornish over the years have espoused the hope that they might be revived.

The adjoining county of Devonshire also had a Stannary parliament, which last met in 1748 when it adjourned to a local public house. As yet there have been no calls for its revival.

A retired Cornish dentist, Dr Nigel Hicks of the now nominal Cornish Stannary, is a vice president of FUEN. His name sits oddly with the largely German speaking central Europeans, which dominate that organisation. At its 2002 congress, the Cornish and Dr Hicks were accepted into FUEN with a motion that read

'As the native Cornish people fulfil the necessary criteria for classification as a national minority, the

FUEN resolves to support the Cornish Stannary Parliament in the name of all Cornish inhabitants. It calls upon the government of the United Kingdom to recognise the Cornish inhabitants as a national minority in line with the Framework Convention for the Protection of National Minorities.'

While welcoming the Cornish, the FUEN noted that although Britain had ratified the Framework Convention, it still had 'a negative attitude'.

So the Cornish joined the ranks of the Crimean Tartars in the Ukraine, the Aromunians in Bulgaria and the Bretons in France, which that same conference had singled out for support.

Dr Hicks was not just a peaceful protester. In January 2002 with two colleagues from the Cornish Stannary parliament he had faced the consequences in court of removing English Heritage signs from 18 historic sites. The three men claimed that English Heritage had no cultural legitimacy in Cornwall.

They had taken down huge English Heritage signs from Tintagel and Pendennis Castles to protest at the use of the word 'English'. Apart from the obvious that they are in Cornwall, there is not much specifically Cornish about either castle: Tintagel is the legendary birthplace of King Arthur but the Normans built the present castle, now in ruins; and King Henry VIII built Pendennis Castle as fort against a Spanish and French invasion threat. Nonetheless, according to a BBC report at the time, a supporter declared the men had made 'the first strike in the Cornish cultural revolution'.

In Truro Crown Court, Judge Graham Cottle said he would make no further comments as 'the publicity is exactly what the defendants seek and I shall deny them that satisfaction.' All three were bound over for a year and had to pay English Heritage £4,500 ($8,000) in compensation.

One odd result of this higher profile for Cornish nationalism was that it encouraged the British government to plan an early referendum for a Regional Assembly in the South West. That plan had to be scrapped when the few interested Cornish realised to their dismay that there was no intention to have a Cornish regional assembly and that the South West region includes five other counties.[2]

The lever of nationality

The Federal Union of European Nationalities (FUEN), which is so keen to promote the Cornish, was established with a benign purpose, but as the decades have passed it has evolved into something more disturbing. While it looks European, even using the EU's ring of gold stars in its logo, it is really German.

The protection of minorities was an issue of considerable unease and disquiet just after the Second World War. Between 1944 and 1948 over 20 million people had been forced to move: their homes had been overrun by armies, or they were the wrong side of a new border. That atrocious period had been preceded by worse barbarities as the armies of both the German Third Reich and the Soviet Union rampaged across Europe.[3]

In 1949, four months after the United Nations General Assembly adopted the Universal Declaration of Human Rights, the Federal Union of European Nationalities was founded in Paris. A French Breton journalist, Joseph Martray, organised that first meeting to promote the rights of ethnic minorities but within a centralised state like France. The French government gave support and sent one of its young state secretaries to attend, François Mitterand, later the French President.

Many of the big names from the French European federal movement were present, nearly all of whom were former socialist resistance leaders, including Dr Hendrick Brugmans and Henri Frenay. Their initial enthusiasm quickly evaporated, and most of them left.

For over 20 years one of the early activists, Povl Skadegård, a Danish civil servant, kept the FUEN alive running annual congresses with some funding from the Danish government, but eventually the debts rose. Germans living in Denmark and the South Tyrol plus Sudeten Germans, paid off those debts. The German government gave occasional overt help: in 1956 it financed the publication of *The Main Principles of Rights for Minority Groups*.

After the fall of the Berlin Wall in 1989 some East European borders, frozen by the Cold War, began to look less stable. The FUEN gained new energy as more associations joined, especially from German and Hungarian minorities in Eastern Europe. By the mid 1990s, when the FUEN needed more money, German groups funded it: they came from Schleswig-Holstein, South Tyrol and Trento, and the Hermann-Niermann Foundation in Germany. Since 1999, a North Schleswig German, Frank Nickelsen, has run the FUEN.

The FUEN's membership of over 75 organisations from 30 countries subscribes to the end of the nation state:

> 'Europe's outfit as the community of sovereign nation states . . . belongs in a museum cabinet for rarities in political history. Its significance in practical politics is crumbling . . . relics of a nation-state era exist in heads, in social structure and state institutions . . . we would be well advised to put them in the right place: they belong to the collective consciousness of the peoples . . . they should be . . . detached from collective identification with states and their power apparatus.'[4]

The FUEN lobbies on behalf of ethnic minorities across Europe. It was the originator of two crucial charters promoting minorities and fronted by the Council of Europe: the *European Charter for Regional or Minority Languages* and the *Convention for the Protection of National Minorities* (see page 154).

Its headquarters is sited in a sensitive area. In 1982 it moved from Copenhagen to Flensburg in Schleswig-Holstein, formerly Danish. Flensburg is the centre of the Danish minority in Germany and only a mile or two from the Danish border.

No doubt that is deliberate, just like the positioning of the first Border Region exactly on the German-Dutch border.

Many in Schleswig-Holstein have not forgotten their history and their Danish ancestry. In 1864 Bismarck's army had attacked Denmark conquering Schleswig and Holstein. Denmark lost a quarter of its fertile land; Prussia took the superb Danish port of Kiel and immediately began to build a naval base used to great effect in both World Wars.

Germany sponsors a Europe of regions
Today, German control of the FUEN is more overt. The German government, the German State of Schleswig-Holstein, and the Hermann Niermann Foundation in Düsseldorf fund the FUEN. The chairman of the Hermann Niermann Foundation, Uwe Stiemke, also works for the German Home Office (Bundesministerium des Inneren) specialising in German speaking minorities. While the German government says there is no conflict of interest that beggars belief.

FUEN's President, Romedi Arquint, explained at the 2002 Congress of Nationalities held appropriately in Subtonic, a Serbian city with a Hungarian culture, why the Congress was focusing on a Europe of regions, not countries.

> 'FUEN has stood for the preservation of lingual and cultural diversity in Europe; even in the founding

phase, it took up the cause of a Europe of regions. Then in post-war years, the old institutions of national states were able to assert themselves.

'This led FUEN to amend its strategy which then fought for the rights of national minorities and defended and demanded federalism as the ideal political structure to establish this diversity; this brought it into discredit with states having central-state rule like France.'

In its 2004 Flensburg Declaration, the FUEN urged the EU Commission to protect minorities, not just in candidate countries, but across the whole EU; to promote minority languages, and to appoint a Commissioner to co-ordinate all this.

In a review of each European country the 2004 FUEN conference demanded

'. . . the government of the United Kingdom to fully implement such measures as suggested by the Council of Europe in support of the Scottish Gaelic, Irish Gaelic and Welsh languages and the Scots and Ulster Scots dialects.

'In addition, FUEN calls upon the United Kingdom government, having recently included the Cornish language within the provisions of the European Charter for Regional or Minority Languages, to take identical measures in respect of that minority language . . .'

All this has encouraged Mebyon Kernow, the Party for Cornwall, to seek a separate assembly for Cornwall with the maximum autonomy possible.[5] Support is low but growing with 3,552 votes in the 2005 general election and just over 2 per cent of the vote in its best constituency.

Germany agitates along its borders

The main target for the FUEN is not Cornwall or indeed the UK. While the FUEN has branches, or what it calls Volksgruppen, in over 30 countries in Europe, including Cornwall, its main area of operations is along Germany's borders. It is also active in all the countries of the former USSR, notably Chechnya and the Ukraine.[6]

In the Czech Republic the FUEN wants to overturn the 1946 Benes Decrees. Under the 1938 Munich agreement Adolf Hitler was temporarily bought off with the annexation of borderlands inhabited by 'oppressed' Sudeten Germans. After the Second World War the Czechs wanted all German civilians to leave with the German troops.

Under the Benes Decrees and backed by the Allies, about 2.4 million Germans were stripped of their citizenship and property without compensation and expelled, unless they could prove that they had been loyal to Czechoslovakia during the war. Czechs regarded their property, including some from thousands of ethnic Hungarians, as war reparations; indeed they were the only reparations Czechoslovakia received.

Not surprisingly even nearly 70 years later the Czechs believe that those who began an appalling war and brutally occupied their country have no case to reverse the expulsions. Germans are welcomed back for visits; local councils tend German graves, but there will be no apologies or return of property. Czech officials point out that 91 per cent of Sudeten Germans voted for a pro-Nazi party in the 1938 elections; they welcomed Hitler's troops. According to the former Prime Minister, Milos Zeman, they were Hitler's Fifth Column. In April 2002 the Czech Chamber of Deputies voted unanimously that the post-war territorial and ownership arrangement was irreversible.

The Austrian and Hungarian governments, both usually German allies, have also demanded the annulment of the Benes Decrees. The FUEN in Hungary, known there as the National Self-Government of Germans in Hungary, backs the FUEN policy. Its president, Otto Heinek, is a member of the Hungarian government and responsible for ethnic minorities.[7]

At first it looked as though the issue of the Benes decrees would hinder the Czech Republic from joining the EU in 2004, but the German plan may be to allow the Czechs to join and put pressure on them afterwards via the European Court of Justice to repeal the Decrees. More Germans would then return to the Czech Republic giving Germany a considerable lever over the Czech government.

Like their neighbours the Czechs, Poles are apprehensive that their new membership of the EU will encourage Germans to re-colonise Poland, particularly Silesia that was part of Germany until 1945, and thus add impetus to German attempts to break Poland up and push Germany's borders eastwards.

Germans are already demanding the return of property seized in 1945. The Chairman of the Silesian Association, Rudi Pawelka, set up a Prussian Claims Society to fight for individual property claims in territories, which today are Polish, Czech and Russian. The Society distributes forms for Germans to claim their property in what it calls 'East Germany' and says it will pursue those claims in the courts all the way to the European Court of Justice.

These German organisations try to deny any knowledge of each other, yet they are intertwined. Erika Steinbach, the President of the Expellees Association, says that the Prussian Claims Society, led by Rudi Pawelka, has no connection with her organisation. That is odd because Pawelka also heads the

Silesian Association, part of Steinbach's organisation. And the deputy president of the Expellees Association is also Pawelka's deputy on the board of the new Silesian Association. And it is based in the Düsseldorf offices of the Landsmannschaft for East Prussia, which backs the scheme.

Erika Steinbach, though not well known at home in Germany, has become something of a hate figure in Poland. She is orchestrating and encouraging German expellees to claim reparations for property they lost in Poland. She so angered Poles that the mayor of Warsaw, Lech Kaczynski, organised a team to calculate systematically the financial cost of the Nazi's destruction of Warsaw. An early estimate was £17 billion ($30 bn), but as the team trawls Warsaw and its archives that figure is likely to soar.

The treaty of Potsdam: how secure are those borders?

In Poland, especially close to the border with Germany, regional movements are growing and are co-operating with German minorities within Poland. The German Interior Ministry is substantially funding these movements and they are spreading to the rest of Poland. Already 2 per cent of the Polish population deny that they are Polish.[8] In the most recent Polish census in 2002 1.25 per cent, that is 173,000 people, registered as Silesian nationals. A further 153,000 Poles described themselves as Germans.

Under the Communist regime the German minority in Poland was small, but from 1989 onwards German minority organisations spread and with them the numbers calling themselves German. It is widely believed that many Poles declared themselves to be German in order to get preferential treatment from the German government.

The German Social Cultural Association began broadcasting German culture in Silesia and within three years the group had organised German instruction in 260 schools, stocked libraries with German books, and arranged technical instruction in Germany for Silesian health and education workers.

That example is being repeated throughout most of Eastern Europe.

One group, the Movement for the Autonomy of Silesia founded in 1990, demands self-rule for the region of Silesia in what it calls a 'Europe of Peoples' (*Voelker*) and with no mention of Poland. Stage one would be the restoration of pre-Second World War autonomy for Upper Silesia, and then later full autonomy within the EU. The Movement wants to stop Upper Silesians leaving for jobs elsewhere and encourages what it calls Upper Silesian exiles in Germany to come back to their Motherland.

The Movement backs the Association of the People of Silesian Nationality but the Polish courts forbade its formal registration because in the Polish constitution there is no such thing as a Silesian nation. The important issue at stake was that if Poland formally recognised the Silesians, then the association could send representatives to the Polish Parliament, even though Silesians are less than 5 per cent of the population, a hurdle every Polish party has to leap. The German-speaking minority in Poland already has this privilege with two deputies in the Polish parliament.

In 1997, the case of *Gorzelik and Others v. Poland* moved briskly through the Polish courts and in 1998, with the plaintiffs on legal aid, it was appealed to the European Court of Human Rights in Strasbourg. In 2004 the Court ruled in favour of Poland.[9] The Court stated

'the Silesians belong to a regional group with a very deep sense of identity, including their cultural identity; no one can deny that they are distinct. This does not, however, suffice for them to be considered as a distinct nation. They have never commonly been perceived as a distinct nation and they have never tried to determine their identity in terms of [the criteria for a "nation"].'

The court accepted that the Polish authorities had acted reasonably, in order to protect the country's electoral system, and unanimously held that there had been no violation of Article 11, freedom of assembly and association, of the Convention for the Protection of Minorities.

Will this setback be temporary only?

The Border Region straddling both the German-Polish (Oder-Neisse) and German-Czech borders is also agitating for German interests in Silesia, Pomerania and the Sudetenland and helping to create the conditions for the German government to put pressure on both the Polish and Czech governments.[10]

A spokesman for the Polish Foreign Ministry, Boguslaw Majewski, has spoken of 'worrying signals' as Germany is increasingly presents itself as a victim of the World War.[11] In September 2003, the then German president, Johannes Rau, accused the victorious powers of the Second World War of 'a dreadful wrong' against Germans 'expelled' from central and Eastern Europe and 'deprived German people of their rights'.

President Rau's remarks implicitly attacked the Potsdam Treaty: the legality of the borders between Germany and it neighbours rest on that treaty. He also attacked those persecuted by the Nazis, who were forced to flee Germany: he charged that while in exile they had 'for years planned the expulsion' of German minorities.

Minorities within Germany itself

Within Germany itself are four ethnic minorities recognised by the German government: Danes, Sintit and Roma, Lusation Sorbs and Frisians. The FUEN has argued for an amendment to the German constitution to consolidate their position. To advance this, the minorities propose to establish a minority committee with a secretariat within the Bundestag. It will be similar to the German minority secretariat within the Danish parliament, the Folketing.

CHAPTER 18

Languages Exploited to Divide Countries

A time machine to the dark ages

Gaelic is dying out. 99 per cent of Scots do not understand a word of it, and the language has been in decline for over a thousand years. Only 58,000 claim to be able to speak it and experts say that when the number of speakers of a language falls below 50,000 it is likely that it will become extinct.

So it is odd to relate that British taxpayers are providing £13.5 million ($24m) every year to boost the use of Gaelic. One primary school in Glasgow is already a Gaelic-only school where every lesson is in Gaelic and the children only start some lessons in English after the first three years. There will be more schools like that. In 2002-2003 1,928 primary and 375 secondary children were taught Gaelic. Another 3,000 children learnt it as a second language. Gaelic is now taught at all levels of education and most importantly as part of teacher training. The lack of Gaelic teachers has been the biggest block to extending its use.

This is all masterminded by the Bórd na Gáidhlig, a board set up by the Scottish Executive in 2003, which has the target of a 5 per cent increase every year in the number of Gaelic medium-educated primary school children. The Board's interest extends to the whole population: today £8.5 million a year ($15.3 m) is spent on producing television programmes in Gaelic.

Or take the case of Manx or Gaelg, a dialect of Gaelic. Manx died out in 1974 but on the Isle of Man, total population only 75,000, there is now a Manx Language Unit, or Yn Unnid Gaelgagh, and several hundred islanders have some knowledge of Manx learnt as adults. Children are taught in playgroups and every child from the age of 8 may learn Manx and take it all the way to 'A' level and university. At one primary school the children learn all their lessons in Manx, just like the school in Glasgow where the children are taught in Gaelic only. Jobs are being created where Manx is used. Everywhere signs in Manx are springing up.

There are over a hundred languages like Gaelic and Manx across Europe usually around national borders. Many of them had virtually died out. How strange then that these local languages and dialects are now being used in public life and taught in schools. In a move calculated to reverse the historical trend very quickly, and within only one generation, much of local life may once again be carried out in these languages.

One source of this is the Council of Europe's *Charter of Regional or Minority Languages*. The 17 signatory countries to the 1992 Charter, which entered into force in 1998, have agreed to revive and promote regional or minority languages because individuals have the right to speak them and to safeguard them from extinction.

Cultural altruism may not be the whole story. Insistence on the use of minority languages arguably may limit opportunities for people in the wider world. It may make them second-class citizens and perhaps easier to control. Their greater use will help to divide countries, not to unite them, and will give regions a greater sense of independent identity.

Another indicator that there may be a devious agenda is that the Charter expressly *promotes* links between minority language groups across national borders and expressly *bars* countries from blocking foreign interference in their national life.

This Charter is hard hitting. It lays out how an official minority language must be used from cradle to grave in every area of public and private life and government funding must be provided.

- Education from pre-school to university, adult courses and teacher training
- Libraries, museums, archives, theatres, cinemas
- Judicial proceedings, employment contracts, product instructions, signs, and safety instructions
- Place names and family names
- Recruiting and training officials and appointing public employees with a knowledge of the language
- At least one radio station, TV channel, newspaper or encourage programmes and newspaper articles
- Funds for the media to use the language and train journalists
- Guarantees not to block the retransmission of radio and TV broadcasts from neighbouring countries in the language

All regional assemblies will have translation services, which will reduce any effectiveness and increase costs.

After Britain signed up

When Tony Blair signed Britain up to the Charter in 2000 and ratified it the following year nearly all regional languages in Britain were either extinct or on the verge of extinction.

In 2004 Denis MacShane, then the Secretary of State for Foreign and Commonwealth Affairs, reported to the House of Commons that

The Government welcomed the Council of Europe's report of 24 March 2004 on the implementation of the Charter for Regional or Minority Languages. The report praises the UK in setting up official bodies for Welsh, Irish and Ulster-Scots. It also applauds the UK for the development of a semi-official body for Scottish Gaelic. The report commends the UK's dynamic approach to the instrument of ratification in recognising Manx and Cornish. It also noted the same approach regarding the ratification for Welsh.[1]

The Council of Europe report encouraged the UK to go further and quicker by

○ Making primary and secondary education in Scottish Gaelic generally available in the areas where the language is used;
○ Establish a system to monitor progress in Scottish Gaelic and Welsh in education, and publish reports on those findings;
○ Provide guidance for teachers and administrators in Scottish Gaelic;
○ Facilitate the establishment of a television channel or a service in Scottish Gaelic and overcome the shortcomings in Scottish Gaelic radio broadcasting;
○ Improve the public service television provision and facilitate the broadcasting of private radio in Irish;
○ Improve the use of Welsh in social care facilities, particularly hospitals and care of the elderly;
○ Create opportunities to use Scots and Ulster Scots in public life.[2]

Britain's six official minority languages
The UK government now recognises six minority languages for the purposes of the Charter: Welsh, Scottish Gaelic, Irish

Gaelic, Scots, Ulster Scots and Cornish. All are being revived, most from near death, and all paid for by the British taxpayer. Manx and Jèrriais, the Jersey patois, are queuing for full recognition.

On the island of Jersey, population 89,000, there were virtually no teachers capable of teaching Jèrriais. Since it was derived from Norman French, some were imported from France. The EU Commission and the Council of Europe together promoted the teaching of these dialects especially in the European Year of Languages 2001.

Welsh has been the most successful minority language within the UK and is the inspiration for the other languages. A quarter of the Welsh population under 35 can now speak Welsh because since 1988 it has been part of the national curriculum. One out of five primary pupils is taught every subject in Welsh. The 1993 Welsh Language Act made it compulsory for children to learn Welsh up to the age of 14. Welsh is a first language for one in seven of all secondary school children, most learn it as a second language.

Parents have so far refused to accept plans for their older children to be taught entirely in Welsh. No doubt they are well aware that speaking in Welsh will help their children to get on in the wider world.

Like the other regional languages, a Welsh language board supervises progress and arbitrarily made the choice of which form of Welsh should be official: so Carmarthen Welsh from the south is in and North Walian is out.

Road signs, signs in public places, the courts and hospitals, are all in Welsh and in English. Translation services must be provided. TV and radio stations and newspapers are all available in Welsh; journalists have language training, at the taxpayers' expense.

While it is not obligatory to speak Welsh in order to get a job in the public sector, which is now over half the Welsh economy, in practice and unofficially preference is given to Welsh speakers. That is the biggest spur of all to the spread of the Welsh language. Some fear that other professional jobs such as doctors may in due course also go to Welsh speakers on the grounds that the patients speak Welsh. So to stay in Wales speaking Welsh may become a necessity. To work outside Wales it will be useless.

Yet even with all that support, the Welsh TV channel, otherwise known as Sianel Pedwar Cymru or S4C, has run into major problems. In 2000 after 18 years of broadcasting it had a mere 7.7 per cent of viewers in Wales. That small number has since fallen by over a third and as reported in the House of Commons

> 'It is now reaching an audience of about the same level as that of Channel 5, despite the fact that 30 per cent. of homes in Wales cannot get Channel 5 at all, and that every home can get S4C.'[3]

Even S4C's programmes in English are being shunned.

There is no doubt that without substantial government incentives Welsh, like the other minority languages, would be on the extreme margins of British national life.

Ulster Scots shows how languages are created

In Northern Ireland a language is being created where once there were simply speakers of a dialect, like most of the other regional languages. Nearly 400 years ago, Lowland Scottish planters introduced this Scots dialect, known as Ullans, to Northern Ireland. A visitor to Northern Ireland would be hard pressed to hear Ulster Scots spoken in restaurants, pubs or shops. Enthusiasts claim 100,000 speakers; the reality is that 30,000 people in Northern Ireland say they can speak some Ulster Scots so it is fast heading for extinction.[4]

To recreate the language and produce a written form, which

has never existed, Ulster Scots now has its own academy. Like the other language boards for Manx, Gaelic and Welsh, it is based on the Académie Française. Tha Boord o Ulster is jointly funded by British and Irish taxpayers to codify the language and the Ulster Scots Institute at the University of Ulster instils academic rigour.

At present the Academy's main pursuit is recording Ulster Scots speakers in their strongholds of Antrim, the Ards peninsula in east Co. Down and east Donegal. The recordings are then analysed to draw up a standard vocabulary. This will lead to the compilation of a comprehensive dictionary and later to a translation of the Bible from the original Hebrew and Greek into Ulster Scots. This will help to standardise syntax, vocabulary and usage.

The academy has launched a newspaper, *The Ulster Scot*, education campaigns and schools' programmes. In some parts of Northern Ireland road signs in Ulster-Scots are springing up, and any government department producing documents in languages other than just English must also issue them in Ulster Scots.

The model for this programme is the Friesian Academy in the Netherlands, which employs 140 full time staff, supplies visiting professors to Dutch universities and already has its Bible completed.

Local people may choose between Dutch or Frisian as their official first language. 350,000 out of 600,000 have chosen Frisian, nearly 60 per cent of the population. Will this be helpful to the future unity of the Netherlands?

Scots still a third class language

Many more people speak Scots as a second language than the other UK languages and dialects – perhaps over 1.5 million people. But Scots, the language of Burns, is not promoted with huge subsidies like Gaelic and Welsh.[5] Under the Charter,

Welsh, Scottish-Gaelic and Irish have the higher of the two levels of Council of Europe recognition: the British government must back the public use of the language. Irish is now the 21st official language of the EU. But Scots is only taught and academic research encouraged: its public use is not yet backed.

Cornish builds a separate identity

In 2002, after a two-year inquiry at taxpayers' expense, the British government recognised Cornish as Britain's sixth official minority language. Cornish is now taught in schools, and some local authorities include Cornish spellings on road and place signs.

The first Cornish language film, *Hwerow Hweg* (Bitter Sweet), was released in 2002. It is described as a contemporary love story of a drug addict and his teenage girlfriend set in West Cornwall. The premiere was held in a House of Commons' committee room: a first for the Houses of Parliament. Andrew George, the Liberal Democrat MP for St Ives, organised the screening. Eva Blassar, editor of Eurolang, flew from Brussels to attend.

Yet Cornish, which had as many as 40,000 speakers in 1066 at the time of the Norman Conquest, is generally accepted to have become extinct as vernacular speech by 1800: the last native speaker died in the 1890s. Today, according to Cornwall County Council, 30 to 50 people can speak Cornish fluently. The Government Office for the South-West (GOSW) recently spent more taxpayers' money to find out that over 2,900 people are able to have a simple conversation in Cornish. Asda, the supermarket, is helping by having signs in both English and Cornish in its local stores.

The British government is caught on the horns of a dilemma. The government is promoting separateness by backing Cornish. By doing so it is gives encouragement to extremists like Dr Hicks and his friends from the Cornish Stannary parliament in their campaign for a Cornwall of the Cornish and down with the rest.

EU defender of minority languages

The revival of some minority languages like Welsh predates the Council of Europe's charter. That is because the Council of Europe is not acting alone in promoting regional languages across Europe. It is in partnership with the EU. The over arching authority within the EU is the Language Policy Unit in the directorate general for Education and Culture.

The EU financially supports over 35 minority languages and began to do so in 1983 both to EU members and to Norway outside the EU. The EU budget to publicise minority languages for 2003 alone was £600,000 ($1.1m).

In 1982 the EU had set up the European Bureau for Lesser Used Languages, now in Dublin, which works with the EU Commission on the *European Commission Action Plan for the Promotion of Language Learning and Linguistic Diversity*.[6]

The Commission claims that regional languages are too important an issue to be left to national governments. It says that allowing the 'local level', that is governments, to control regional and minority languages will only strengthen the stronger languages and endanger the weaker ones. The Commission promotes itself as the defender of the weak.

The Commission also set up the Eurolang News Agency in Brussels. It is less of a news agency, more of an information-gathering organisation and monitors the use of languages across Europe.

To promote minority languages especially in schools and universities, the Commission set up and funds Mercator in three centres, Liouwert in the Netherlands, Barcelona in Spain, and the University of Wales in Aberystwyth. They advance the policies of both the EU and Council of Europe to protect ethnic minorities, minority languages and equal citizenship.

They also provide research for the EU's Bureau for Lesser Used Languages. Bizarrely, according to the Mercator website, they actively promote conflict resolution, though the website fails to give examples of such conflicts.

France awake to the dangers

There is no doubt that the language policy of the Council of Europe and the EU can help to divide and fragment countries, and that may be the intent. Across Europe nearly every country has at least four minority languages, and the bigger the country the more the languages. Italy for example has 11.

France has recognised the very considerable problems that the Charter could cause. A 1999 report written for the French government listed no less than 75 languages, which would qualify for recognition.[7] There are 28 minority languages within France, 10 of them spanning the French border into neighbouring countries, plus a very large number in French overseas territories (35 in New Caledonia alone).

President Chirac took the issue to the French Constitutional Council in July 1999. The Court ruled that the *Charter of Minority Languages* was incompatible with the French Constitution, which enshrines French as the language of the Republic. For the moment this potential challenge to the borders and integrity of France has been resisted.

The role of Germany in a fragmenting Europe

There may be yet another agenda to the promotion of minority languages. German is a minority language in nearly all the countries close to Germany's borders: in France, Belgium, Denmark, Estonia, Finland Hungary, Czech Republic, Italy, Poland, and Slovakia. Promoting German within those neighbouring countries could be construed as beneficial to an expansionist Germany.

German is likely to be the major and deliberate beneficiary

of the Charter in Europe despite the fact that English is the world's leading language, over five times as many people speak it compared to German.

Indeed the EU claims that German is the number one language in Europe with over 92 million speakers. In contrast, English is an official second language in Malta alone. The EU ignores the fact that English as a foreign language is much more widely spoken than German.[8]

The German language bias to the Charter is also emphasised by its history. It was a German from the Federal Union of European Nationalities' legal committee, Herbert Kohn, who launched the *Charter of Regional or Minority Languages*. To build on this Charter, in 1996 the German government founded and pays for the European Centre for Minority Issues or *Europaeisches Zentrum fuer Minderheitenfragen* (ECMI), almost next door to the FUEN offices in Flensburg, Schleswig-Holstein.[9]

While Germany itself has over 20 minority languages, oddly the German ECMI acknowledges just five of them: Low German, Danish, Frisian, Romany, and Sorbian (popularly known as Wendish).[10] These languages are spoken on and across Germany's borders with Denmark, the Netherlands, the Czech Republic and Poland.

The other languages, like Swabian, are 'internal' within the boundaries of Germany and of no use to extend Germany's reach into a neighbouring state. Arguably, therefore they are not part of a German plan.

So the intent behind promoting minority languages might not only be an issue of divide and rule. It could well be that the expansion of German influence into neighbouring countries is part of the agenda behind the advancement of minority languages.

CHAPTER 19

How Far is Germany Implicated?

'A disastrous road'

Regions as we have seen are not a British invention. Regions are the European Union's form of local government. British regions and British regional assemblies are without any doubt just parts of a division of the whole of the EU and its applicant countries into regions as required in the treaty of Rome and the acquis communautaire.

Yet the deeper the investigation into regions goes the more the words Germany and Germans come to the fore. Arguably the German Länder are the blueprint for the regions into which Britain and the rest of the EU have already been divided.

The Cornish language has been revived from near death – as well as Gaelic, Scots, Manx and Jèrriais – because of a Council of Europe Charter launched by a German. Some Cornish claim recognition as an ethnic minority backed by a German organisation, the FUEN, in Schleswig-Holstein. Dr Hicks, one of the FUEN's vice presidents, and his friends went so far as to 'strike a blow for Cornwall' by demolishing English Heritage signboards, no doubt encouraged by this overseas' interest.

Britain has two vast Border Regions encompassing the counties of Kent and West Sussex and crossing the English Channel.

It was Germany, which invented the concept in the 1950s and developed the first Border Region, EUREGIO. Today every part of Germany's borders is within a Border Region.

Since none of these things is home grown in the UK and no nationals other than Germans are implicated in their origins, it is fair to assume that Germans, and probably the German state itself, are the source. If so, Germany must see national advantage in regional government and regional identity both of which over time, and with the help of the EU, will help to break up nation states across Europe.

For many in Britain, a German policy of supremacy or hegemony in Europe is so unpalatable that it is ignored, avoided or buried. It smacks of extremism and stereotyping, which as a nation the British rightly avoid. We should take heed, however, when Germans themselves sound the alarm. They know their country. Relatively few British speak German well or visit that country compared with the British love of France and the Mediterranean countries. Ten times as many British holiday every year in both France and Spain as go to Germany.

Here is one well-placed German sounding that alarm. Walter von Goldendach, the pseudonym of an author 'associated' with the German Foreign Office, wrote in 1997,

> 'German politics has embarked on a disastrous road and is on the verge of carving up Europe into ethnic regions, the idea being that the remains of the crushed nation-states will orbit around the great power that is Germany. The earlier this strategy is opposed, the smaller the sacrifice which will probably have to be made in resisting Germany's claim to power.'[1]

Much of what follows in this chapter is evidence of German planning of a kind in which Anglo-Saxon countries do not indulge and therefore causes some disbelief. Germany has an approach to governance, which is removed from Anglo-Saxon ideas of freedom, tolerance and laissez-faire. But as Sir Oliver Wright wrote in a different context,

> 'When Ambassador in Bonn, I was frequently instructed to get an off-the-cuff reaction to a new development. I had as often to explain that the Germans did not do off-the-cuff reactions. What they had was a *Gesamtkonzept*, an overall framework of policy. After much serious thought they would incorporate the new development into a modified *Gesamtkonzept* which they would then expound at great length.'[2]

German expansion disguised

Germans, who are deliberately exploiting the wish of ethnic minorities for recognition to help break up other European countries, are building on a concept of race and nationality developed over the last hundred years or more, with roots that can be traced back three centuries.

The old German idea of *Staatsvolk,* invented to protect property rights in what was then a feudal society, developed into a *Volk,* a community sharing both heredity and culture and superior to all other peoples. An individual cannot survive unless bound to the *Volk* or community. That tragically led to aggressive anti-Semitism, because the Jews were regarded as a foreign and inimical 'race'.

Under both Chancellor Otto von Bismarck and Kaiser Wilhelm II, the idea of *Volk* as the basis to define the state became part of foreign policy. Influential organisations, like the Pan-German Union and the Society for German Culture Abroad, manipulated German-speaking minorities, outposts of Germany in other countries. They spread the *Volk* ideology using it to justify Germany's claims and thus to expand its political and economic influence into neighbouring countries. The 'right to self-determination' defined in terms of *Volk*, allowed Germany to weaken other countries and to further German domination.

This was the nub of the Irredenta Policy, which during the Weimar Republic (1919 to 1933) backed German minorities abroad inciting them to undermine the sovereignty of other nations. To do this the German Foreign Office and other government departments created a substantial machine, government financed but operating as a network of private societies, avoiding overt association with the German government.[3]

Adolf Hitler and the National Socialists took over that machine. A network of research institutes drew up plans to justify the right of German *Volk* groups abroad to be integrated into the German Empire. For example, in 1938 the Nazis used the excuse of German minorities to annex the Sudetenland, part of Czechoslovakia. To achieve the necessary *Volk-transformation*, they carried out mass murder, particularly of Slavic peoples and the Jews.

Post war, to safeguard national boundaries and prevent a rebirth of the *Volk* group undermining other countries, Germans still living in the former German eastern territories were resettled, notably from Silesia which became Polish.[4]

But out of the public eye and protected by German state officials, the old *Volk* activists re-grouped. In effect, they pursued an additional foreign policy under the umbrella of the German Foreign Office and the Ministry of the Interior. They revived the Society for German Culture Abroad (Verein für das Deutschtum im Ausland or VDA), and the Pan-European Union (PEU), and created German Societies of the Expelled (see page 160).

All these organisations tried to disguise their German

nationalist goals by including the aim of a federal Europe under the umbrella of the EU or the EEC.

Germany expands using the EU and the Council of Europe

After the fall of the Berlin Wall in 1989, the revolution in Eastern Europe created new opportunities for German foreign policy. After forty years of necessary constraint in pursuing German goals in Eastern Europe, Germany is again using German-speaking minorities as levers. Just as after World War I, German foreign policy is using overtly independent organisations.

Again, institutions are camouflaged as European, but they only partly hide their German interests. Their involvement, ostensibly for human rights in foreign countries, may further a German goal of continental hegemony.

Using the Council of Europe and German charitable foundations, Germany has steadily worked towards five (so far) important conventions. Each gives powers to ethnic minorities and regions within countries and takes power away from nation states. It is not a highly visible assault against the integrity of sovereign countries but a gradual erosion over time.

The five Conventions or Charters are:

1 *The Framework Convention for the Protection of Minorities*
2 *The Convention on Transfrontier Co-operation between Territorial Communities or Authorities, the Madrid Convention*
3 *The Charter of Local Self-Government*
4 *The Charter for Regional or Minority Languages*
5 *The Draft European Charter of Local Self-Government*

A careful examination shows that the guiding hands behind all these conventions are German, ostensibly to 'protect' minorities in countries other than Germany and to enable those minorities to 'associate' across national borders. None of them appears to originate from the German government: they are described as European but only Germans were originally involved.

1 Minorities must be protected

The first convention, *the Framework Convention for the Protection of Minorities*, can be traced back to at least 1956. The German dominated Federal Union of European Nationalities (FUEN) wrote it and tried for many years to get other countries to accept it. It took over thirty years for the Council of Europe to come to an agreement, which it did in 1993. Siegbert Alber MEP, a prominent German lawyer who has since become an Advocate General at the European Court of Justice, broke the deadlock by putting the more contentious issues, those on human rights and autonomy for minorities, on one side. Five years later the Convention came into force.

The UK is a signatory and has agreed to protect ethnic minorities within the UK, enabling them to develop their own culture and keep their own ethnic identity.

2 Regions have their own foreign policy

The second convention, known as the *Madrid Convention*, enables regions to have their own independent foreign policy, separate from the countries of which they form a part.

Members of the Association of European Border Regions (ARBE) wrote the *Convention on Transfrontier Co-operation between Territorial Communities or Authorities*. To call the ARBE 'European' is misleading: it too is German. Its founders and organisers all come from the Rhineland.[5] For the last 15 years its secretary general has been a German, Jens-Dieter Gabbe, and its first four presidents were German. The headquarters is at Gronau, near Enschede, exactly and deliberately on Germany's border with the Netherlands, echoing the careful positioning of the FUEN in Schleswig-Holstein. Gronau is also the headquarters of the very first Border Region (see page 149).[6]

In 1965 Alfred Mozer, the German instigator of the first Border Region, chaired a group to plan the Madrid Convention with representatives from the four German Border Regions, which embrace parts of France, the Netherlands, and Switzerland.[7] Dr. Viktor Freiherr von Malchus wrote the key report, *Cross-border co-operation in Europe*.

In June 1971, the first meeting of the Standing Committee of European Border Regions (10 regions in all) was held at Anholt Castle, again symbolically on the German-Dutch border, and the Convention was launched later that year in Bonn. It was finally agreed in 1980 in Madrid.

The Madrid Convention encourages border agreements between regions from adjacent countries.[8] It gives model agreements for just about every form of co-operation imaginable, especially planning, down to such minutiae as park management and the use of riverbanks.

Two protocols in 1995 and 1998 strengthened it. One recognised the right of regions within nation states, 'territorial communities', to make agreements across national borders, which would have to be recognised in domestic law. All those co-operation bodies would have legal personality.

The second protocol gave regions the right to have a foreign policy independent of their nation states: that is to make agreements between regions that are not adjacent.

This is a major attack on the integrity of sovereign countries.

The UK is not yet a signatory. 33 other European countries have ratified it, though they have not all signed the strengthening protocols.

Across the EU, the *Madrid Convention* has been recognised in national legislation. For example:

○ In 1992 the Joxe Act authorised French regions and local authorities to conclude cross border agreements and organisations.
○ Denmark has a number of agreements including the 1993 Oresund Region Transborder Co-operation between Copenhagen and Malmo in Sweden, two cities now joined by a bridge partly funded by the EU.
○ In 1997 Scandinavian countries agreed the Baltic Sea States Subregional Co-operation.
○ In 1998 the Belfast Agreement included cross border organisations.

3 Regions self-governing within the EU

The Charter of Local Self-Government, launched in 1981 and agreed in 1985, backs the right of local people to run an important part of their public affairs, with sufficient financial resources, and with legal protection. Another German, Dr A. Galette from Schleswig-Holstein, wrote the report, *Regional Institutions in Europe*, on which the charter is based.

This convention allows all regions to be self-governing, obviously to the detriment of the nation state. Yet self-government would be an illusion: instead of regions within a nation state, the regions would be subordinate to the European Union.

Successive French governments hesitated to adopt this charter. Were they to do so, France would be divided into regions, which have not existed since about the year 1000. France did sign in 1985 but for the next 20 years failed to ratify the Charter. In January 2004 the French government announced that it had begun the ratification process.

The British Conservative Government under John Major declined to sign the Charter. As Earl Ferrers for the government remarked in the House of Lords

We have a long tradition of effective local government—a tradition which is founded on, and which is given practical expression by, the legislative decisions of your Lordships' House and of another place. We do not need a European convention to bolster those traditions or to show that we carry them out.[9]

One of the first acts of the new British Labour government in 1997 led by Tony Blair was to sign the charter and then ratify it a year later.

4 *Germany pays for minority languages to break up nations*
As discussed in chapter 18, a German from the Federal Union of European Nationalities' legal committee, Herbert Kohn, launched the *Charter of Regional or Minority Languages*. In 1996 the German government founded and is paying for the European Centre for Minority Issues or *Europaeisches Zentrum fuer Minderheitenfragen* (ECMI), almost next door to the FUEN offices in Flensburg, Schleswig-Holstein that promotes the Charter.

The German government is promoting German culture, the German language and German education in all its neighbouring countries but especially in Eastern Europe and on a scale unknown to other Western governments.

Curiously the form of German taught is almost exclusively Hoch Deutsch or High German in contrast to the proliferation of minority languages and dialects being promoted in every other European country.

5 *The next step, landerisation of Europe*
Still in draft, *The European Charter of Regional Self-Government* reflects the depth of German planning on regions. Its architects again come from the strategically important and sensitive Rhineland.

In 1997 a Council of Europe working group launched the principle of the landerisation – or regionalisation – of the whole of Europe. The plan had strong backing. The group's chairman, Peter Rabe, was a member of the Diet of Lower Saxony of which Chancellor Gerhard Schröder was then the President.

This Charter has been held up because many countries are still unwilling to agree to their own regions directly applying to the European Court of Justice and by-passing national justice. Meanwhile EU funded lobby groups like CALRE and REGLEG are the paid chorus to hasten agreement to the Charter (see page 136). Work continues.

EU Constitution supported regions

Not surprisingly, the EU Constitution continued the long battle to destroy nations by promoting regions. While the Constitution itself has been dropped, its constituent parts may still be promoted.

An influential German think tank, the Centre for Applied Political Research (CAP), funded by the Bertelsmann Foundation based in Gutersloh, and working closely with the German Foreign Office, claims that regions have acquired 'more bite' with their new powers and that they should strive to strengthen their position. It judges that regions are in a critical stage of their development. Regions, says the Bertelsmann Foundation, can now legitimately demand comprehensive integration into the EU decision-making process.[10]

The Constitution included the following:

○ The EU has to respect its own 'rich cultural and linguistic diversity': the two main characteristics of regional identity, Article 1–3

○ Local and regional self-governments are 'fundamental structures' to be respected by the EU, Article 5–1

○ For the first time the Committee of the Regions was to be
  given the right to bring limited actions before the
  European Court of Justice.[11]

Germany tries to guarantee its integrity
The 16 German Länder are in the process of being bound to
Berlin's political direction. A federal commission from both
houses of the German parliament has been set up to modernise
the federal state. It is expected to cut the influence of the
Länder by changes to the constitution 'so Germany may be
better and more simply governed'.

That raises the important question of why Germany appears
to be going in the opposite direction to all the other countries
of the EU. There may indeed be an unpublished agenda in
Berlin, which is at odds with its public support for the
regionalisation or landerisation of Europe.

Who put regions into the treaty of Rome?
At the beginning of this book we saw that it was the treaty of
Rome, which enabled the Commission in Brussels to develop
the idea of regional economic government, which today
encompasses far more than just the economic, and to which
each new member country has to agree. So who wrote those
clauses into the 1957 treaty?

The 1956 draft of the treaty of Rome, called the Spaak
Report, only mentioned regions twice. Yet one year later, the
final treaty contained a preamble and many clauses cleverly
designed to sound the ultimate death knell of nation states.

No written evidence has yet come to light on who masterminded those clauses. Germany's part in writing the 1957
treaty of Rome is not well understood and it is not known if
Germany was responsible, though by a process of elimination
it was the most likely country to have done so.

Six countries negotiated the treaty of Rome. Of those six,

France was the least likely to want regional government, which would destroy its highly centralised constitution. Indeed that has been seriously resisted. It is difficult to imagine that Italy, Belgium, or the Netherlands, let alone tiny Luxembourg, would want regionalisation. On the other hand socialists from any of these countries would probably have been in favour.

So for the moment it has to remain an educated guess that the German team, led by Hans von der Groeben who shortly afterwards became the first EEC Commissioner for Competition Policy, was the proponent of regions in the treaty of Rome.

Regions are to the benefit of Germany alone. Germany, the only country in the EU which has not had to change its local government structure, was probably the only country with not only the interest but also the will.

CHAPTER 20

In Conclusion

Decision-making will be closer to the people, the British government claims in its White Paper on devolving power to the UK regions, *Your Region, Your Choice.*

> 'More democracy, less bureaucracy . . . new opportunities, new powers and new choice.'

Yet the British government also states that regions should only 'as far as practicable be democratically accountable'. To the parish councils the government says it wants to change 'from a representative democracy to a consultative democracy.'

More democracy, less democracy: those views are contradictory. Both cannot be true. The British government has been playing Jekyll and Hyde. It is two faced.

All the evidence from the new regions, sub regions and sub sub regions is that the British government is abandoning democracy and transparency, while substantially increasing bureaucracy and taxes. A revolution indeed!

By introducing the foreign idea of unelected 'stakeholders' who lobby for commercial firms, trade unions, churches and charities, and embedding them in regional government; by introducing proportional representation leading to party control of candidates on party lists, and to coalitions of parties;

and by replacing open and transparent councils of equals with cabals, the Labour government's actions speak louder than words.

The Labour government's perverse actions include using millions of pounds of taxpayers' money to fund so-called independent think tanks and lobby groups that present only one side of the argument for regional government. Archbishops and bishops of the Church of England back regions and so do charities working for clear political ends.

While the actions of the Blair government in riding roughshod over the British electorate have gone far beyond those of any other government in modern times, earlier governments, both Labour and Conservative, have increased the power of central government to the detriment of local government and local democracy.

Entwined with this loss of democracy there is another agenda, that of the European Union. When the British government signed the treaty of Rome in 1972, like all EEC member states it was legally obliged to introduce regions with borders defined by the EEC and intended ultimately to break up nation states. That commitment to introduce regional government was not obvious until the EU expanded in 2004 to take in Eastern European countries, all of whom had to change their systems of local government before joining.

The governments of both Harold Wilson and Edward Heath were guilty of grave deceit when they disguised the EEC's condition for regional economic government and tried to introduce it as though it were wholly British. Then John Major's government gave the EU a substantial lever with the creation of Government Offices in each region. John Major disguised the true purpose behind that policy.

But it is under Tony Blair's leadership that the disappearance of Britain has dramatically speeded up. His government has weakened democracy, railroaded referendums with token public debate, and conducted a rotten referendum in Wales. No doubt he has done so in the belief that the Labour Party will become the natural party of government and to entrench its position, but it is almost certain to fail.

By accelerating the destruction of British local government and replacing it with the EU's system of local government, the Labour Party is destroying British independence and the United Kingdom.

What the Labour government calls the New Localism, its revamped parish councils, and the Market Towns Initiative are both helping the EU to penetrate to the lowest possible level of government, even influencing such truly provincial matters as bus routes, signs outside railway stations and the local golf club.

The campaign to recognise a Cornish ethnic minority and the Cornish language along with Gaelic, Manx, Welsh and the rest should ring more alarm bells, though no doubt most people would not immediately link them with either the EU or an attack on the integrity of the nation state.

The EU's paid sycophants, some of them in the UK, are calling for the next stage of the revolution, to enable regions to appeal over the heads of national government to the European Court of Justice. Will a British government aid that too?

It is bad enough that any British government should attack and diminish democracy as Tony Blair's government has done. It is worse that a British government should hand powers over local government to the European Union and without being straight with the British people.

There is an even greater concern, which has only begun to be obvious in the years after the fall of the Berlin Wall. The power behind the campaign for regions, border regions, ethnic minorities and languages across the whole of Europe is the troika of the German government, German foundations and German institutes.

Countries surrounding Germany know only too well that over the centuries Germany's borders have gone in and out like bellows. The countries of Eastern Europe in particular are understandably nervous of the potential for German hegemony. They are worried about the integrity of their borders, which were fought over, for which millions died, and which have been in place only for a relatively short time. Their concern should be the concern of everyone across Europe, a Europe that could still become a German Europe.

We are not privy to the detail of the latest *Gesamtkonzept* developed in Berlin, but we should note the evidence of it: evidence that demonstrates German interference in national life across the whole continent of Europe.

Britain should not be a pawn in this dangerous game, let alone aid and abet it. A British government should lead the way. Democracy must be restored and enhanced at every level of local government. The EU's regional government must be eradicated. The size of central government must be sharply reduced. Those are the surest ways to secure freedom for everyone.

If a British government fails in this critical task, as it is failing today, every council and every county, town and parish councillor can help or even pre-empt this process by withdrawing from regional government and refusing to fund it.

Harder to do but no less necessary, every council should turn its back on EU grants with their hidden agenda. Take the money and you take the EU's terms of business too.

If the British fail to eradicate the EU's regional government with its many tentacles entwined around so much of our national life, it will indeed be the case of Disappearing Britain and the arrival on our shores of a foreign totalitarian government which the Allies with 'blood, toil, tears and sweat' defeated in two long world wars.

Notes and References

Introducing the Slow Death of Nations and Democracy

[1] Jacques Delors, French economist and politician, who served three terms as President of the European Commission 1985–1995, speaking to the European Parliament, July 1988

[2] See *The Last Days of Britain, The Final Betrayal*, Lindsay Jenkins, 2001

[3] 31 May 2005. In 2005 the British had to work for an extra three days for their government compared with the year before

[4] A public meeting held by Chepstow Council, reported by Greg Lance-Watkins, the complainant

[5] *The Daily Telegraph*, 1.2.2005

[6] Yorkshire Today, 2.2.2005

[7] The ODPM published a series of documents: *The Future of Local Government – Developing A 10 Year Vision*, July 2004; *Vibrant Local Leadership*, 2005 a 35 page paper; *Citizen Engagement and Public Services: Why Neighbourhoods Matter*, January 2005, 41 page report; *Sustainable Communities: People, Places and Prosperity – A Five Year Plan from the Deputy Prime Minister*, 2005; *Strengthening the role of local leadership, Factsheet one*, 2005; *Putting more power in the hands of the community, Factsheet two*, 2005; *'How to' guides on Cleaner, Safer, Greener Communities, Factsheet three*, 2005; *Mixed Communities Initiative, Factsheet four*, 2005; *Local area agreements, Factsheet five*, 2005; *Case studies*, 2005

[8] John Redwood by email, 14.1.2005

[9] *Review of letters to the local press*, by Josephine White. Carried out over a week in early December 2004

[10] *The Yorkshire Post*, 16.10.2004. Since the Yorkshire and Humber Regional Assembly receives 35 per cent of its funds from local councils, it contritely replied that it would halve its subscription rate

[11] At the time of publication the Conservative controlled Cheshire County Council had given one year's notice to the NW Regional Assembly of its withdrawal. The Labour controlled Lancashire County Council withdrew in 2004

Chapter 1: Voters Resoundingly Reject Regional Government

[1] The British government planned to hold referendums in three regions on the same day. Fear that the voters might reject at least those in the North West and in Yorkshire and Humberside led the government to 'postpone' them. The North East referendum went ahead even though public interest there, like the other two, was negligible. The referendum was held under the Regional Assemblies (Preparations) Act, 2003

[2] *The Journal*, 11 Oct 2004

[3] Hansard: 8 Nov 2004: Column 588

[4] Hansard: ibid.

[5] www.odpm.gov.uk, 2004

[6] First Report of Session 2004–05, 'The Draft Regional Assemblies Bill', January 2005

[7] Nick Raynsford in a letter to Cllr Bransby Thomas, Chair of the English Regions Network, 21 February 2005

[8] Hansard: 10 Nov 2004: Column 839

[9] www.richardcorbett.org.uk, 2005

[10] www.cec.org.uk/press/myths/myth67.htm, 2004

[11] In conversations with the author

Chapter 2: The EU Defines Regional Government

[1] The original six member countries were Germany, France, Italy, the Netherlands, Belgium and Luxembourg

[2] *Regionalism and Parliament*, G H Jones, B C Smith and Prof HV Wiseman, *Political Quarterly* No 38, 1967

[3] Article numbers are those in the original treaty of Rome, not as amended by subsequent treaties

[4] The European Parliament was not elected until 1979

[5] *Première Communication de la Commission sur la Politique Régionale dans la Communauté Économique Européene* II/SEC(65) 1170 final, Commauté Economique Européenne Commission, 11 May 1965

[6] ibid. Introduction

[7] ibid. p 39

[8] ibid. p 41. Treaty of Rome, articles 129 and 130

[9] www.eib.org, 2004

[10] *Britain and the EEC Regional Policy*, Hugh M Begg and J Allen Stewart, *Political Quarterly*, No 44, 1973

[11] The Financial Instrument for Fisheries Guidance and the Guidance Section of the European Agricultural Guidance and Guarantee Fund

[12] *Une politique régionale pour la Communauté*, Commission des Communautés Européennes, 1969 Translated by the author

[13] Article 2 of the Treaty of Rome

[14] *Une politique régionale* op. cit. p 61ff

Chapter 3: Regionalising Britain is a Long Term Project

[1] Local Government Act, 1888 established 62 elected county councils, including London County Council, and 61 all-purpose county borough councils in England and Wales.
Local Government Act, 1894 revived parish councils and set up 535 Urban District Councils, 472 Rural District Councils and 270 non-county Borough Councils.
London Government Act, 1899 set up 28 metropolitan borough councils in London and the Corporation of London.

[2] Social Insurance and Allied Services, VI, 1942–3

[3] 1951 Manpower Committee
1959 Pritchard Committee on Rating of Charities
1959 Roberts Committee on the Library Service
1960 Herbert Commission on Greater London
1962 Willink Commission on the Police
1965 Allen Committee on Rates
1967 Mallaby Committee on Staffing in Local Government
1967 Maud Committee on Management
1968 Seebohm Committee on the Social Services
1969 Skeffington Committee on Public Participation

[4] Hansard: 10 Nov 2004: Column 839

[5] George Brown, later Baron George-Brown (1914–1985). Deputy

leader of the Labour Party under Hugh Gaitskell, he challenged for the leadership after Gaitskell's death, but was defeated by Harold Wilson. In 1964, Wilson appointed him Secretary of State for Economic Affairs; he instituted price and wage controls. Made Secretary of State for Foreign Affairs in 1966, he resigned in 1968 after a long battle with alcoholism.

[6] Report of the Royal Commission on Local Government, Cm 4040, 1969. Lord Redcliffe-Maud (1906–1982), former diplomat

[7] H of Lords Deb. vol 334, col 59, July 31 1972

[8] Although called two-tier, the system was really three-tier, as it kept parish councils

[9] *The Sunday Times*, 11 July 1971

[10] FCO 30/387, Rippon letter, 23 July 1971

[11] FCO 30/837, from Notes for Supplementaries, 26 July 1971

[12] Lord Wheatley chaired the Commission. Its report published in 1969 led to the Local Government (Scotland) Act, 1973

Chapter 4: Who Masterminded the Regional Revolution?

[1] The Fabians take their name from the Roman general, Quintus Fabius Maximus, the Delayer, who defended Rome against Hannibal by elusive tactics and avoiding pitched battles

[2] Politicians' links with the Fabian Society are seldom noted. In the 1906 House of Commons the Fabians held 29 Liberal seats and 42 Liberal seats in 1911. After their switch to the Labour Party in 1919, 10 Fabians sat in the 1922 parliament. 47 won seats for Labour in the 1929 election with 19 government posts. In the 1930s, the numbers fell, but with Labour's landslide victory in 1945, over half the Labour MPs were Fabians, 229 including 10 Cabinet Ministers, 35 Under Secretaries, 11 Parliamentary Private Secretaries

[3] For a full discussion of the role of the Fabian Society in the creation and development of the EEC see *Britain Held Hostage, The Coming Euro Dictatorship* Lindsay Jenkins, 1998, pp 33ff

[4] *Fabian Socialism*, G D H Cole, 1943

[5] *The Story of Fabian Socialism*, Margaret Cole, 1961

[6] See *Fabian Thinkers, 120 years of progressive thought*, edited by Ellie Levenson et al for the Fabian Society, 2004

[7] www.spg.org.uk, 2004

[8] Sir Bernard Crick is Emeritus Professor of Birkbeck College, University of London, and an Honorary Fellow, Edinburgh

University. First taught at Harvard, then McGill returning to teach at the LSE from 1956-1967. First professor of Politics at Sheffield 1967–1973, thereafter at Birkbeck. Publications include *The Reform of Parliament, In Defence of Politics, Orwell: a Life, Political Thoughts and Polemics, Essays on Citizenship, Democracy: a very short book*. Writing *The Four Nations*. For many years editor of *The Political Quarterly*, joint founder of the Study of Parliament Group, first president of the Association for Citizenship Teaching. Reported to the Home Secretary on education for naturalisation in 2003 as *The New and the Old*. Adviser on Active Citizenship to the Home Office 2003–04

[9] Royal Commission on the Constitution 1969–1973, Cm 5460

[10] Prof. John P Mackintosh, 1929–1978 *The Government and Politics of Britain*, 1968

[11] House of Lords debate, Hansard: 21.3.2001: Column 1454

[12] Devolution within the UK (Cm 5460, 1974); Democracy and Devolution (Cm 5732, 1975); Our Changing Democracy (Cm 6348, 1975); Devolution to Scotland and Wales (Cm 6585, 1976)

[13] *Devolution: The End of Britain?* Tam Dalyell, 1977. Dalyell, educated at Eton and Kings College Cambridge, was MP for West Lothian from 1962 to 2005

[14] 52 per cent voted Yes and 48 per cent No. But only 32.9 per cent of the total electorate voted Yes

Chapter 5: The UK is Broken Up

[1] The 1985 Local Government Act abolished the Labour controlled metropolitan counties and the Greater London Council. Unfortunately Mrs Thatcher made local authorities largely dependent on central government funding, thus almost eradicating local democracy

[2] *Observing Subsidiarity*, LGIU Briefing, July 1997

[3] The Local Government (Scotland) Act 1994

[4] See also the Labour Party's *Renewing the Regions: Strategies for Regional Economic Development*, 1996 and *A Voice for England's Regions*, 1996

[5] In *The Future of the European Union*, a report on Labour's position in preparation for the Intergovernmental Conference 1996. First presented at the Labour Party Conference in Brighton on 2 October 1995

[6] *Scotland's Parliament*, Cm 3658, July 1997, *A Voice for Wales*, Cm 3718, July 1997

[7] ibid. Annex J

[8] *A New Deal for Transport: Better for Everyone*, Cm 3950, 1998

[9] *Your Region, Your Choice*, p 70

[10] John Prescott speech, Manchester, 22 January 2004

[11] John Major, the Prime Minister, Speech at the Lord Mayor's Banquet, 14 November 1994

[12] *Standards in Public Life, The Funding of Political Parties in the United Kingdom*, Cm 4057, 27 July 1998. Fifth Report §12.32

[13] ibid. vol 1, p 163

[14] The Regional Development Agencies Act. The RDAs are: Advantage West Midlands, East of England Development Agency, East Midlands Development Agency, London Development Agency, NorthWest Development Agency, One NorthEast, South East England Development Agency, South West of England Regional Development Agency, and Yorkshire Forward

[15] There is also the Highlands and Island Enterprise

[16] The Greater London Authority Act, 1999

[17] Hansard: 14 Dec 1998: Column 625

[18] *Your Region, Your Choice: Revitalising the English Regions*, Cm 5511, 8 May 2002

[19] *Alice Through the Looking Glass*, Lewis Carroll, ch 6

[20] *Your Region, Your Choice* §2.27

[21] *Your Region, Your Choice* §6.6

[22] *Your Region, Your Choice* §9.6

[23] Directorate of Policy and Development www.nwra.gov.uk, 2003

[24] www.are-regions-europe.org, October 2002

Chapter 6: Churchmen and Charities Campaign for Regions

[1] The Scottish Constitutional Convention was chaired by Sir Robert Grieve, previously chairman of the Highlands and Islands Development Board, the main agency to develop the Scottish Highlands. Its secretary was Jim Ross, a retired Civil Servant who had played a prominent part in drawing up the previous bill for a Scottish Assembly prior to 1979

[2] *The Future South West*, 19 May 2001

[3] ibid. p 30

[4] ibid. pp 9–11

[5] Private correspondence with Tony Bennett, August 2002

[6] Hansard, 21 March 2001: Column 1430

[7] Among the extensive literature see *England: The State Of The Regions* Ed. John Tomaney and John Mawson, 2002. One example of a unit within a university is the West Midlands Governance Action Research Group

[8] www.yes4theNorthEast.com, 2004

[9] From Pam Barden's *Save Our Sovereignty*, a privately circulated newsletter

[10] *A Soul for Europe* aims to give 'a spiritual and ethical dimension to the European Union.' Jacques Delors, a former President of the European Commission, started it. See europa.eu.int, 2004

[11] Treaty establishing a Constitution for Europe, CIG 87/04, 6 August 2004

[12] www.regionalfutures.org.uk, 2004

Chapter 7: How Taxpayers Pay to Persuade Themselves

[1] Hansard: 19 May 2004: Column 1048W

[2] www.cfer.org.uk, 2004

[3] www.jrf.org.uk, 2004

[4] The Devolution and Constitutional Change Programme was set up by the ESRC in 2000 to explore the devolution reforms, which have established new political institutions in Scotland, Wales, Northern Ireland, London and the other English regions since 1997. Over 30 research projects were selected to dissect the implications of devolution for the UK state, society and economy. See www.devolution.ac.uk, 2004

[5] www.emra.gov.uk/topics/documents/ERN_key_messages.pdf, 2004

[6] www.SouthWest-ra.gov.uk/swra/ourwork/ern/index.shtml, 2004

[7] Hansard: Written Answer, 19 May 2004: Column 1043W

[8] E.g. *The Future of EU Regional Policy post 2006* or *L'avenir de la Politique régionale de l'UE après 2006, Points de Vue du réseau des régions Anglaises*

[9] www.civicforum.org.uk, 2004

[10] Hansard: 24 May 2004: Column 1434W

[11] Pam Barden's Save Our Sovereignty Newsletter

[12] Hansard: 23 Jan 2003: Column 487

[13] Hansard: 5 Mar 2003: Column 802

Chapter 8: Regions have Limited Powers

[1] www.regionalassemblies.co.uk, 2004

[2] See in particular the Committee of the Regions publications e.g. COR Studies 1 1/2001–16 May 2001

[3] *The Times*, 29 April 2002

[4] *European Spatial Development Perspective* (ESDP), Part A1 *The Spatial Approach at European Level*, p 5, (Potsdam, May 1999)

[5] *Planning: Delivering A Fundamental Change*, Department for Transport, Local Government and the Regions, December 2001. Now The *Planning and Compulsory Purchase Act*, 2004

[6] *Your Region, Your Choice* op. cit. §2.26

[7] See *Britain Held Hostage, The Coming Euro-Dictatorship*, p 251

[8] In the South West this initiative is called the Market and Coastal Towns Initiative, and in Scotland the Small Towns Initiative.

[9] www.southwesttowns.net, 2004

[10] Rural White Paper: *Our Countryside: The Future – A Fair Deal for Rural England*, Cm 4909, November 2000

[11] The Countryside Agency is funded by the Department for Environment, Food and Rural Affairs (Defra), with an annual budget of around £100 million ($180 m), and over 600 countryside specialists and support staff in the Cheltenham and London head-quarters plus in offices in all the regions. The Agency is a develop-ment of the Rural Development Commission (1909) and the National Parks Commission (later the Countryside Commission) set up in 1949

[12] Hansard: 29 Oct 2002: Column 732W

[13] See *The Last Days of Britain, The Final Betrayal* Lindsay Jenkins

[14] From their foundation in 1994 until 2000, the Government Offices represented three Whitehall Departments. Further development was outlined in the report *Reaching Out*, February 2000. Since then, there has been a major change: in 2003 the number of Departments that the Government Offices represent increased to nine. Departments such as the Home Office, the Department for Environment, Food and Rural Affairs and the Department for Transport have reorganised and strengthened their regional teams. They all have staff working in the Government Offices

[15] Cm 5808 *Our Fire and Rescue Service*, 30 June 2003

[16] *Justice for all: Criminal Justice White Paper*, Cm 5563, July 2002 Courts Act 2003

[17] Hansard: 4 Nov 2003: Column 776

[18] Letter in *The Times*, 21 August 2003 from a number of retired Judges: 'The proposed change effectively tears the heart out of the existing circuit . . . Removing Hampshire from the Western Circuit would . . . reduce the number of circuit judges from 56 to 37, the number of district judges from 46 to 30, and the number of Crown Courts (the court rooms, not the buildings) in round figures from 50 to 30. The number of barristers practising on the circuit would be drastically reduced, perhaps by more than one half. Amputating Hampshire would threaten the viability of the entire Western Circuit . . .'

[19] Hansard: 4 Nov 2003: Column 777 and 778

[20] www.scottishdevelopmentinternational.com, 2005

[21] The issue of block grants (now known as DEL) to maintain the United Kingdom, and in particular the 1978 Barnett formula for Scotland, now looks as though it is an EU issue and not a UK issue but has not been publicly addressed, let alone resolved

[22] www.richardcommission.gov.uk, 2005. ISBN 0 7504 3184 9

Chapter 9: Taxpayers Foot a Heavy Bill

[1] Debate, Manchester, 22.1.2004

[2] National Audit Commission report

[3] Hansard: col. 658W, 18 November 1998. Humberside plus eight districts was created in 1974, abolished in 1996 and returned to the East Riding of Yorkshire and to Lincolnshire and the districts replaced by four unitary authorities

[4] *Your Region, Your Choice* §8.19

[5] www.ccre.org, 2005

Chapter 10: Democracy Redefined and Downgraded

[1] *Your Region, Your Choice* §7.11

[2] Local Government Act, 2000

[3] *Your Region, Your Choice* §2.26

[4] Mrs Suzman, the well known South African anti-apartheid campaigner and former Member of Parliament, was commenting on the abandonment of the first-past-the-post electoral system in South Africa in *The Sunday Telegraph*, 16 May 2004

[5] The PR system used in UK regional elections is the Additional Member System (AMS), just as it is for the German Länder. Each

voter has two votes. The first vote elects a constituency member by the first-past-the-post method. The second vote elects 'top-up' members on a party list system.

[6] EU 'Systems and Services for the Citizen' Directorate www.cordis.lu/ist/ka1/administrations/projects/projects2.htm, 2004

[7] *From Ballot Box to Fiasco*, The Ballot Box Society, July 2004

Chapter 11: Cabals Challenge People Power

[1] Hansard: 14 Dec 1998: Column 623

[2] The source of this quotation requested anonymity

Chapter 12: Stakeholders Diminish Democracy

[1] Report to County Councils scrutiny committee, August 2004

[2] The Essential Guide to British Quangos 2005, Dan Lewis, CPS

[3] At 31 March 2004, the latest available date, there were 839 public bodies sponsored by UK Government departments: 2 Nationalised Industries, 9 Public Corporations, the Bank of England, 24 NHS Bodies and 803 NDPBs. The NDPB group is made up of 210 Executive NDPBs, 407 Advisory NDPBs, 34 Tribunal NDPBs and 152 Independent Monitoring Boards. www.knowledgenetwork.gov.uk, 2005

[4] www.2wm.co.uk, 2005

[5] www.cultureNorthEast.org, 2004; www.livingeast.org.uk, 2004

[6] The Countryside Agency, a government quango, designates National Parks under the National Parks and Access to the Countryside Act, 1949

[7] For a fuller discussion of the role of Federal Trust see *Britain Held Hostage, The Coming Euro-Dictatorship*, Lindsay Jenkins pp 109, 231, 232

[8] *Encouraging Democracy and Stakeholder Participation in the English Regions*, Federal Trust, 2003 page 9

Chapter 13: Sub Regions 'Respond to a Strong Regional Voice'

[1] *The Future of Local Government: Developing a Ten Year Vision*, The Office of the Deputy Prime Minister, July 2004

[2] ibid. p 6

[3] SI no 2001/2812

[4] Department for Environment, Food and Rural Affairs: White Paper *Our Countryside: The Future, A Fair Deal For Rural England*

Chapter 14: New Regions Envelop Europe

[1] *Your Region, Your Choice* op. cit §6.3, 6.4

[2] europa.eu.int/comm/eurostat/ramon/nuts/basicnuts_regions_en. html, 2004

[3] Regulation (EC) 1059/2003, 26 May 2003

[4] The EU has also defined countries in a Commission Decision (91/450/EEC, Euratom, 26 July 1991): a country according to the EU includes embassies and military bases overseas, oil and gas deposits, air space and territorial waters. One might wonder why the Commission has taken this step

[5] CoR Studies I – 1/2001–5, Brussels, June 2001

[6] L'éditorial du Monde La France girondine, *Le Monde*, 4 Oct 2002

[7] Charles Maurice de Talleyrand – Perigord, 1754–1838

Chapter 15: The EU Spins across a Continent

[1] www.cor.eu.int, 2004

[2] *Birmingham Post*, 8 February 2002. Bore was the CoR president from 2002 to 2004

[3] *Accountacy Age*, 1 August 2004

[4] www.calre.net, 2004

[5] www.coe.int/T/E/CLRAE, 2004

[6] www.calre.net, 2004

[7] www.regleg.org, 2004 and Summit of the European Council held in Laeken, Belgium

[8] Preamble to the Convention setting up the Council of Europe, ETS 001, 1949

[9] Aberdeen, Argyll and Bute, Cornwall, Devon, East of England Regional Assembly, East of Scotland Consortium, Fife, Gloucestershire, Hampshire, Highland, Isle of Wight, Isle of Man, Northern Ireland Association, Orkney, Scottish Parliament, Shetland, Somerset, South of Scotland Alliance, Western Isles

Chapter 16: 'Borders are the Scars of History'

[1] atlas-transmanche.certic.unicaen.fr, 2005

[2] The Mikado, *I've Got a Little List*

[3] Interreg IIIA website, www.interreg.org, 2004

[4] www.regiontransmanche.com; www.kent.ac.uk/economics/ research/interreg/ComparativeStudy.pdf

[5] For example: 1963 Rein-Waal Agreement crossing German and

Netherlands borders; 1991 cross border treaty between Germany and the Netherlands for cross border contracts; 1996 Karlsruhe Agreement between Germany, France, Luxembourg and Switzerland for cross border co-operation at regional and local level; 1998 Dreier Landtag agreement between South Tyrol (Austria) and Trentino (Italy) and the Land Tirol on cross border co-operation.

[6] *The Rise of the Euroregion A bird's eye perspective on European cross-border co-operation*, Markus Perkmann, Lancaster University, www.comp.lanc.ac.uk/sociology/papers/Perkmann-Rise-of-Euroeregion.pdf, 2005

[7] EUREGIO, Germany/Netherlands, 20.1.1981

[8] Alfred Mozer 1905–1979 Former Head of Cabinet at the European Commission

[9] The Zentrum Group, the foremost group in the Rhineland, was apolitical but wished to guarantee the rights of the Roman Catholic Church in Germany. Its reputation was for total expediency to promote the Rhineland even against other parts of Germany, notably Prussia

Chapter 17: Manipulating Minorities to Divide and Rule

[1] Förderalistische Union Europäischer Volksgruppen (FUEV), www.fuen.org, 2004

[2] Pam Barden's SOS publication, op. cit.

[3] For a detailed review from the First World War to the end of the Second World War see chapter 5 of *Facing History, The Evolution of Czech-German Relations in the Czech Provinces, 1848–1948* published by the Czech Ministry of Culture

[4] ibid. History of the FUEN

[5] Memorandum by Mebyon Kernow, the Party for Cornwall (DRA 35), evidence to Select Committee on Office of the Deputy Prime Minister: Housing, Planning, Local Government and the Regions, 21 July 2004

[6] www.fuen.org, 2004

[7] In 1998 there were 271 German minority self-governments in Hungary, 30 were municipal governments with mayors from the German minority. The National Self-Government of Germans in Hungary has 10 regional offices. There are 3 independent German high schools and more schools have German faculty classes. There are many hundreds of German societies in Hungary, most have been

set up in the last 25 years. 200 German settlements are twinned with towns in Germany or Austria and close ties with Germany. In 2002/3 the Andrassy Gyula University in Budapest was opened with instruction in German partly financed by the German government

[8] There were also 48,700 Belorussians, 31,000 Ukrainians, 12,000 Roma people, 1,100 Jews, 1,100 Armenians, 8000 Czechs, 500 Tartars and 50 Karaims

[9] The Case of Gorzelik And Others v. Poland (44158/98) [2004] ECHR 72 (17 February 2004)

[10] For one view sympathetic to integration see *The German-Polish Border Region. A Case of Regional Integration?* Jorunn Sem Fure, University of Bergen, ARENA Working Papers WP 97/19

[11] European Foundation Intelligence Digest, 18-30 June 1998

Chapter 18: Local Languages Exploited to Divide Countries

[1] Hansard 19 May 2004: Column 1085W

[2] Recommendation RecChL(2004)1 of the Committee of Ministers on the application of the European Charter for Regional or Minority Languages by the United Kingdom

[3] Hansard 27 May 2004: Column 1765

[4] Northern Ireland Life and Times Survey, 1999

[5] Hansard 17 Jan 2001: Column: 233W

[6] www.eblul.org, 2004

[7] Report author was Bernard Cerquiglini

[8] *Euromosaic: The production and reproduction of the minority language groups in the European Union*, EU Commission, 1996

[9] *Europaeisches Zentrum fuer Minderheitenfragen* (ECMI) www.ecmi.de, 2004

[10] The centre also promotes 'universal, regional, bilateral and national standards that may assist in consolidating democratic governance on the basis of ethnic diversity and human rights.'

Chapter 19: How Far is Germany Implicated?

[1] A valuable, rare and brave insight on the German issue is presented by Walter von Goldendach and Hans-Rüdiger Minow, in *Von Krieg zu Krieg* (From One War to the Next), 1999 ISBN 3-931745-03-1 See also web site www.german-foreign-policy.com

[2] Sir Oliver Wright GCMG GCVO DSC, *The Salisbury Review* (Book review), Spring 2004

[3] Irredenta literally means a region that is related ethnically or historically to one country but is controlled politically by another

[4] Silesia formally became part of the German Empire in 1871, many Germans moved there. Poles were then about 30% of the population. The 1919 Treaty of Versailles gave Upper Silesia a plebiscite: about two thirds voted to be part of Germany. But the southeast, the economic backbone, voted for Poland. After three Silesian Insurrections, the League of Nations split the province: areas that voted for Poland became autonomous within Poland and the rest reorganised within the Prussian provinces of Upper and Lower Silesia. In October 1938 Poland retook the disputed area West of the Olza river from Czechoslovakia, in accord with the Munich Agreement. In 1939 Germany attacked Poland regaining those parts of Silesia. Silesian Poles were killed or deported, and Germans took their homes. In 1945 Soviet troops occupied Silesia. Under the 1945 Yalta and Potsdam agreements, most of Silesia east of the rivers Oder and Neisse was transferred to Poland. Most Silesian Germans were forcibly expelled. After the war, Silesian industry was rebuilt, more Poles moved there (mainly those expelled from lands annexed by the USSR). Today more than 20% of the Polish population live in Silesia.

[5] Much of Rhine Province, a former province of Prussia 1815–1919, also known as Rhenish Prussia or the Rhineland, was under Allied armed occupation after 1919 until Hitler's army reoccupied it in 1936. Today the northern section (including part of the industrial Ruhr) is in the state of North Rhine–Westphalia, and the southern section (with its wine districts along the Moselle and Rhine rivers) in Rhineland-Palatinate

[6] www.aebr.net, 2004

[7] CIMAB – Alsace and Breisgau, EUREGIO, Regio Basiliensis, and Regio Rhein-Waal

[8] European Outline Convention on Transfrontier Co-operation between Territorial Communities or Authorities, CETS 106, 1980

[9] Hansard 18 Nov 1996: Column 1156

[10] www.freenations.freeuk.com, 2004

[11] Article 7, Protocol on the Application of the Principles of Subsidiarity and Proportionality, Draft Treaty establishing a Constitution for Europe, 2004

Index

Also by Lindsay Jenkins:

Lindsay Jenkins

Britain
Held
Hostage

With a dramatic new
foreword by
Frederick Forsyth

The history of the European Union. Who created it and why

The Last Days of Britain

The Final Betrayal

Lindsay Jenkins

Foreword by Norman Lamont

The story of how Britain surrendered to Europe